Democracy, Governance and Economic Policy:
Sub-Saharan Africa in Comparative Perspective

John Healey and Mark Robinson

ODI Development Policy Studies

Democracy, Governance and Economic Policy

Sub-Saharan Africa in Comparative Perspective

John Healey
Mark Robinson

Overseas Development Institute

A CIP catalogue record for this book is available from the British Library.

ISBN 0 85003 171 0

Published by the Overseas Development Institute, Regent's College, Inner Circle, Regent's Park, London NW1 4NS

Typeset in Postscript by Jane Kennan at ODI.

Printed by the Russell Press Ltd, Nottingham.

Printed on recycled paper.

Acknowledgements

We would like to acknowledge help from a number of people whom we consulted, especially Teddy Brett, Reginald Green, Michael Lipton, James Manor, Mick Moore and John Toye at the Institute of Development Studies at the University of Sussex; John Dunn and Geoffrey Hawthorn at the University of Cambridge; Catherine Cameron, Rosalind Eyben, Garth Glentworth, Ken Gubbins, Pat Holden, Barry Hudson, Brenda Killen, John Roberts, Peter Sandersley and Brian Thomson at the Overseas Development Administration; Denis Osborne at the Royal Institute of Public Administration; Robert Cassen, Derek Robinson and Lawrence Whitehead at the University of Oxford; Garth Armstrong of the Crown Agents, and various colleagues at ODI, especially Tony Killick. We are also grateful to Sandra Finlayson, Geraldine Healy, Jane Kennan, Claire King and Patsy de Souza for typing various drafts of the manuscript and to Margaret Cornell for her valuable editorial assistance. An earlier version of this monograph was prepared with support from the Overseas Development Administration, which we gratefully acknowledge. Responsibility for the views expressed here rests with us alone.

J.M.H.
M.R.

Contents

Preface

The timing of this monograph reflects a recently renewed interest, especially among international and bilateral aid agencies, in the political dimensions of development and in what constitutes 'good government' in the Third World.

The study is primarily addressed to those administrators, diplomats, economists and other professionals concerned with the day-to-day business of development who may not have the time to keep abreast of the work of political scientists, sociologists and historians, much of which has relevance to the current interest in political regimes and the political processes which bear on economic policy-making and economic performance in developing countries. It is based on a wide-ranging review of relevant parts of the literature in the fields of politics, political economy and policy analysis. The main focus is on sub-Saharan Africa but more general work on developing countries is also covered in order to put African experience and prospects into a wider context.

The aims of the study are fourfold:

- First, to review the evolution of authoritarian rule in sub-Saharan Africa since independence, interpretations of the state and its decay, and various classifications of African political systems (Chapters 1-3).
- Second, to examine political explanations of economic policy formation and change in sub-Saharan Africa in the 1970s and 1980s (Chapters 4-5).
- Third, to review the state of the academic debate on democracy and development in the Third World, the arguments and research evidence on the relationship between political regime type on the one hand, and the character of economic policy and performance on the other, and the implications of regime type and changes in the political system for economic adjustment policies in the 1980s (Chapters 6-7).
- In the final chapters (8-9), contemporary political and economic change in sub-Saharan Africa is evaluated and some attempt is made to assess the prospects for political liberalisation and greater political accountability in the light of Latin American

experience. The likely implications of such political developments for economic management are tentatively explored in the concluding chapter.

Summaries of the main conclusions are provided at the end of each of the first three Parts.

A glossary of terms and concepts employed in the political science literature is provided at Annex 1; this is designed for those who may not be familiar with the terminology used in this study.

The literature on such a wide set of issues is extensive and often diffuse. For this reason the review has had to be selective. Since it has only scratched the surface there may well remain highly relevant research work and perceptions which do not feature. We point to certain areas for research which appear to be neglected (Annex 2) and hope that our initial efforts will provoke others to correct or modify our perspectives. Finally, our review convinces us that there is much more scope for fruitful joint work between political and economic analysts.

Part I

Sub-Saharan Africa:
Political Evolution since Independence

1
The Emergence and Consolidation of Authoritarian Rule

A salient feature of the politics of sub-Saharan Africa for most of the period since independence has been the persistence of highly personalised authoritarian rule. Various explanations have been put forward in the literature to account for the demise of democratic institutions in the post-colonial era. Earlier interpretations focused on external political factors associated with economic dependence. In the 1980s it became increasingly common to attribute growing problems of governance and economic malaise to the internal characteristics of authoritarian regimes. This introductory chapter begins with a brief review of the legacy of colonial rule and the types of regimes that emerged during the process of decolonisation. It then examines the trend towards authoritarian rule and the reasons for the prevalence of the one-party state as the dominant idiom of post-colonial politics.

Politics at independence

There are two competing interpretations of pre-colonial politics in Africa: one that authoritarianism and hierarchy formed the basis of traditional rule, the other that traditional African societies were essentially democratic, with extensive consultation taking place and decisions being reached by consensus (Kunz, 1990). As Hodder-Williams points out (1984:12-13), both of these are caricatures, and neither was universally applicable. In reality there was enormous variation in traditional African politics, ranging from societies governed by hierarchical structures through to those characterised by dispersed authority and consensus-building. To some extent these reflected underlying socio-economic factors, such as resource endowment and population densities, although the precise political arrangements emerged from complex societal processes. Despite such variation there existed a rich body of constitutional practices in pre-colonial Africa, defined by reciprocity, accountability and a form of political legitimacy by which rulers could be challenged if they transcended established cultural and political norms (Gluckman, 1965).

Colonial rule in some cases supplanted traditional political institutions by force, whereas in other societies pre-colonial forms of rule formed the basis for imperial hegemony, in which existing political leaders collaborated with the colonial authorities in return for the preservation of their power and status (Lonsdale, 1981; Hodder-Williams, 1984).

During the first few years of independence many observers were optimistic about the prospects for enduring democratic rule in Africa. This view was underpinned by the expectations aroused by the allure of self-determination and the credentials of nationalist leaders who had used democratic arguments to press for an end to colonialism. In a number of countries, especially those formerly governed by Britain and France, liberal constitutional arrangements had been created during the twilight years of colonial rule to facilitate the transfer of power, although these were subject to protracted bargaining and consultation between the colonial rulers and nationalist leaders before agreement was reached.

In Ghana and Nigeria constitutional reforms prefaced the introduction of regional self-rule and competitive elections in the early 1950s (Chazan, 1988; Diamond, 1988b). A territorial assembly was created in Senegal after 1946 followed by the progressive introduction of universal suffrage (Coulon, 1988). Some have argued that these constitutional provisions allowed for greater African participation in political life and instilled democratic traditions which have persisted, albeit haltingly, to the present day, forming the basis for a revitalised politics (Diamond, 1988a; Kunz, 1990). As Young (1988) has observed, both the departing colonial authorities and the nationalists used the liberal democratic framework of the metropolitan state as the authoritative blueprint for the post-colonial regime, even though this was at odds with the autocratic traditions of the colonial era.

However, the benign aspects of the colonial inheritance should not be overstated; the dominant characteristic of colonial rule was autocracy, enforced by repression (Crowder, 1987). It was only in its later phase that constitutional reforms were implemented, often to stem the rise of radical nationalism and the installation of regimes which would be strongly averse to maintaining linkages with the former colonial powers (Collier, 1982; Young, 1988). These reforms were introduced with little regard for the indigenous political culture and in many cases ensured the dominance of a political elite which had only very tenuous links with the broader mass of the population.

Nonetheless, the majority of countries which achieved independence in the early 1960s were ostensibly committed to a liberal democratic political system, with regimes coming to power by means of competitive multi-party elections. In countries such as Ghana, Kenya and Tanzania, nationalist movements institutionalised themselves as political parties, and assumed a commanding position in national politics following the departure of the colonial regime (Post, 1968; Collier, 1982).

The founders of the post-colonial African states were often charismatic individuals who believed that they had earned the right to rule by virtue of their prominence in the struggle against colonialism (Zolberg, 1968). Most of them shared two overriding objectives: to achieve the goals of modernisation, thereby fulfilling popular expectations, and to maintain themselves in office. Nationalist leaders also shared an implicit belief in the ease of engineering social change once representative institutions had been established within a liberal democratic framework. They hoped that their people would shed pre-existent ethnic allegiances and identify wholeheartedly with the modern, secular values of the post-colonial state (Doornbos, 1990).

However, there was greater differentiation in the character of nationalist movements than was originally realised in the 1960s, and this conditioned the form of rule in the post-colonial period. For instance, there was a striking difference between nationalist movements which achieved independence through a peaceful transfer of power and revolutionary nationalist movements which achieved independence through protracted military struggle. Many nationalist leaders were wedded to socialist ideologies which inclined them towards the one-party state, ranging from the populist African socialism espoused by Presidents Nyerere of Tanzania and Kwame Nkrumah of Ghana through to the Marxist-Leninist doctrine favoured by the regimes which came to power in Angola, Mozambique and Ethiopia in the mid-1970s (Young, 1982).

The rise of authoritarianism

Contrary to the expectations of the more optimistic observers, the experience of liberal democracy in independent Africa proved to be short-lived. Within a few years of achieving independence, the trend had shifted in favour of authoritarianism, with the elimination of political competition and the creation of one-party states either by constitutional fiat or by military takeover.

In several countries, elected governments were responsible for eliminating democracy by means of what Diamond (1988a) terms 'executive coups'. In Senegal this process found expression in the gradual erosion of legislative authority, the concentration of executive power and the outlawing of opposition parties (Coulon, 1988). In Ghana, a highly centralised presidential system was legitimised by a national referendum in 1960 which laid the basis for an increasingly repressive one-party state headed by Kwame Nkrumah (Apter, 1963; Chazan, 1988). Milton Obote in Uganda accomplished the transition to authoritarian rule by changing the constitution and crushing the political opposition through the use of force (Diamond, 1988a).

Jackson and Rosberg (1982:23-4) have summarised the process as follows:

> Modern African authoritarianism is characterised by the removal of constitutional rights and protection from political opponents, the elimination of institutional checks and balances, and the centralisation and concentration of state power in presidential offices, as well as the termination of open party politics and the regulation and confinement of political participation - usually within the framework of a single ruling party.

They identify three mechanisms which were used to disarm the opposition or to secure co-operation from ethnic and regional interest groups: (i) co-optation and consultation, (ii) patronage entailing the exchange of state resources in return for political support and (iii) agreement to perform or desist from performing particular activities, such as organising public rallies against the regime. Autocratic or dictatorial rulers tended to resort to coercive methods to enforce compliance, while in the more open oligarchies a combination of these measures was employed.

In other countries the eclipse of democratic rule was much more abrupt and bloody as a result of military intervention. In Nigeria, civilian rule ended with a military coup in 1966 and the assassination of the prime minister and a number of regional politicians and senior military officers (Luckham, 1971). Since then there have been a number of successive coups with only four years of democratic government (Diamond, 1988b). In contrast, in Ghana military intervention in 1966 had the effect of reversing the authoritarian tendency already present in the First Republic, although a subsequent coup in 1972 led to the installation of a repressive military regime (Austin and Luckham, 1975). Many other countries followed a similar path, with military intervention becoming an institutionalised mechanism for political succession (Bienen, 1978). Several countries experienced a series of coups, with military regimes characterised by conflicting ideological orientations or differing ethnic composition coming to power (Gutteridge, 1975; Decalo, 1976). By 1984 half the countries in Africa were ruled by military or quasi-military governments and a further third by one-party governments or hereditary monarchies (Sandbrook, 1986:322).

The shift towards authoritarianism from the mid-1960s was justified on the grounds that a strong central state was necessary in order to further the objectives of nation-building and economic modernisation, especially in view of ethnic and communal divisions. Traditional forms of decision-making which laid stress on patrimonial authority were also used as a justification for the one-party state. Such views found ready support among academic observers of various ideological hues who believed that Western democratic forms were inappropriate or at least unrealistic in view of the absence of pre-conditions such as widespread literacy and industrialisation (Hodder-Williams, 1984:114-22; Staniland, 1986:55-62).

Yet in spite of the trend towards authoritarianism, several one-party regimes maintained a high level of popular participation during the mid-1960s (Bakary, 1990; Mutahaba, 1990). According to Hodder-Williams (1984:119), 'Factionalism within the party was deemed preferable to structured antagonism between separate parties vying for power'. Moreover, competitive parliamentary and local elections in one-party regimes such as Tanzania, Kenya and Zambia provided voters with an element of choice, even though there were limits on the scope for dissent from the official party line. To underline the point, Coleman and Rosberg (1964) drew a distinction between pragmatic-pluralistic regimes such as those in Tanzania and Zambia, and the revolutionary-centralising party, which was characteristic of countries such as Guinea and Congo, where constraints on opposition activity were absolute.

However, by the late 1960s, most of these semi-competitive one-party states had become increasingly authoritarian. Nationalist leaders were concerned with achieving national unity while at the same time retaining power, and this entailed a routinisation of the charismatic authority established during the heady days of the struggle against colonialism. Those in power tried to consolidate their control over civil society by reducing the scope for opposition activity and curbing the independence of trade unions, co-operatives and other interest groups (see Chapter 5). Nationalist parties became entrenched political monopolies which provided rewards to individual or group claimants in the form of political office or public sector employment (Zolberg, 1968; Young, 1982).

As Callaghy (1986:32) observes, single-party regimes proved to be an instrument not of mobilisation but rather of control and incorporation. In the process they drew on the coercive methods favoured by the colonial states, the principal features of which were the control of pluralism (through inclusion within the single party or exclusion by military dictatorships), the strengthening and extension of centralised administrative structures, and highly personalistic forms of rule using eclectic brands of legitimising doctrines.

Only a handful of countries managed to distance themselves from the authoritarian trend. Botswana, Mauritius and The Gambia are virtually unique in Africa in having retained competitive multi-party systems since achieving independence, although all three are special cases, and differ in many ways from the larger African states.

Unlike most countries in Africa, the Tswana tribes in Botswana share a similarity of language and cultural traditions. The dominant ethnic group has pursued a strategy of accommodation with other groups which has in turn encouraged political stability. Effective local government has widened political participation and the traditional communal assemblies are consulted by the government before development policies are implemented (Molutsi and Holm, 1990). Botswana has the added advantage that it is rich in minerals and other natural resources which has made it easier to put the economy on a sound footing (Harvey and Lewis, 1990). Nevertheless, the country has been ruled by the same party since independence, giving rise to a situation of one-party dominance under a paternalistic English-speaking elite (Stevens and Speed, 1977; Wiseman, 1977; Holm, 1988).

The reasons for the preservation of a democratic political system in The Gambia are less clear. Part of the explanation lies in the fact that independence was negotiated by peaceful means. Political parties were formed relatively late, for the most part representing co-opted elite interests (Perfect, 1986). A single party with a strong rural base has dominated the political scene since independence, and a coup attempt in 1981 was overturned with Senegalese military assistance (Sallah, 1990).

In Mauritius, the first moves towards multi-party democracy were made in the terminal years of colonial rule. There was a peaceful transfer of power at independence in 1968, and with the exception of the early 1970s when political activity was largely proscribed, democratic norms have been maintained. As a contemporary observer of Mauritian politics has noted, 'the acceptance of democratic procedures has brought a degree of political stability to Mauritius that is rare in the developing world' (Bowman, 1991).

Mauritian politics are characterised by what Bowman has referred to as a 'seamless web' of consolidation and fragmentation among the major political parties and an endless parade of alliances and pressures within the ruling party, reflecting a multiplicity of pressures based on class, religion, race, caste and language. The key reasons for this persistence of multi-party democracy lie in the political culture of the country and the success of Mauritian economic development. More specifically, Bowman lists the following factors: a common spoken language but official support for all languages; the absence of a national army; consensus over a mixed economy (at least since 1982); widespread agreement over the desirability of multi-party democracy; political leaders subject to intense public scrutiny; corruption and nepotism kept under control; and radical political activity given an outlet via constitutional channels. Clearly, the combination of all these factors has favoured democratic politics since independence. Although it is very different from most countries in mainland Africa, the experience of Mauritius shows that ethnic and linguistic cleavages are not inherently inimical to multi-party democracy; in the final analysis, the way that such cleavages are channelled and mediated depends to a large extent on the skill and dexterity of political leaders.

In search of explanations

The demise of democratic government in sub-Saharan Africa raises questions about its failure to thrive. In attempting to provide an explanation Diamond (1988a:5) lists a number of contributory factors: political insecurity, ethnic divisions, weak political institutions, a shallow sense of nationhood, limited managerial and technical talent, extreme economic dependence and unfulfilled popular expectations. To this list Callaghy (1986:33) adds particularistic pressures (sectional and communal), high birth rates, rapid urbanisation, and expectations of rapid change generated by the ideological and policy pronouncements of the nationalist leadership. Zolberg (1968) argued that the newly independent states lacked the power, resources and legitimacy to deal effectively with these challenges.

Although Jackson and Rosberg (1982) maintain that relative social stability has been achieved under personal rule, Sandbrook (1986) argues that political instability is endemic to personal rule in some countries, as reflected in a continuous succession of coup attempts and regime changes. In a similar vein Decalo (1985) points to the persistence of social and cultural cleavages and enduring problems of public order following the overthrow of tyrannical governments in Uganda, Equatorial Guinea and the Central African Republic. These political realities appear to bear out Zolberg's (1968) observation that political instability is an intrinsic feature of post-colonial African states because of their failure to develop effective political institutions to mediate between the state and interest groups within civil society.

Zolberg argued that competition between rival ethnic and regional groups vying for control over state power and resources was the prime cause of political instability after independence. This was especially true in countries possessing 'centralised ethnic systems' such as Nigeria, Uganda and Zimbabwe, where a small number of ethnic groups compete for political dominance, with the result that ethnicity provides a constant reference point for national politics (Diamond, 1988a:10-11). In Nigeria, political instability arose from ethnic conflict exacerbated by a flawed federal structure, which provided the pretext for military intervention. As Decalo (1985) has noted, the single party became the preferred option for governing divided societies. In contrast, in societies characterised by 'dispersed ethnic systems' there are many ethnic groups, and where no single group predominates (as in Tanzania, and to a lesser extent, Ghana) political compromise and co-operation tend to be the outcome rather than conflict and instability. This results in a situation where parties and governments are formed by a process of bloc-building from regional and ethnic coalitions (Rothchild and Foley, 1988). However, the disparate political outcomes in multi-ethnic states would suggest that ethnicity is only one among a number of explanations for authoritarian rule.

There is also the related question of national unity, which featured as a dominant concern in the political lexicon of nationalist leaders after independence. The territorial boundaries of most post-colonial states were artificial constructs, which conformed more to the administrative and political imperatives of colonial rule, but which divided ethnic groups and gave rise to new regional and linguistic cleavages (Jackson and Rosberg, 1988). The consequence was that several regimes had to deal with secessionist movements after independence which challenged their claims to national unity. A centralised administrative and military apparatus was often justified on this basis. Revolutionary regimes which came to power through armed struggle (as in Angola and Mozambique) were themselves faced with the need to combat insurrections (backed militarily by outsiders) which challenged their monopoly of power and gave vent to the authoritarian trend already implicit in their centralising ideologies (Young, 1982:84-95).

Diamond (1988a:13) places some of the blame for democratic failure on the shoulders of the political leadership, the majority of whom, he argues, were only weakly committed to liberal democracy. He draws attention to the ease with which nationalist leaders were prone to abuse power and ignore basic democratic norms and procedures. He infers that most leaders upheld democratic conventions during the period of decolonisation as a means to achieve independence rather than as a guide to political behaviour in the post-colonial period. However, cautioning against culturally deterministic explanations of democratic failure, he claims that democratic values were not completely or uniformly lacking, and that such values help to explain the persistence of the democratic ethos in countries such as Botswana and Senegal.

Lonsdale (1986:145) makes the point that the African inheritors of the colonial state found access to power too easy and straightforward. Instruments of political control and economic allocation had already been constructed by the colonial powers. No hard lessons of discipline were learned by the new rulers and the need to mobilise popular support never arose in the way that, for example, Indian politicians had to face in the years before independence.

Another set of factors were the inauspicious economic circumstances of most African states: they were generally characterised by low levels of development, widespread poverty, poor resource endowment, small domestic markets, heavy dependence on a limited range of primary exports, and vulnerability to external shocks.[1] These factors restricted their political leaders' room for manoeuvre, and limited the extent to which they could fulfil popular expectations through economic modernisation and in the process raise living standards. This resulted, in turn, in a growing gap between the ideological perceptions of rulers and their capacity to implement the necessary policies. Growing disenchantment provoked a response in the form of authoritarianism in order to contain popular pressure, or provided popular support for military intervention. External political factors also played a role in that foreign powers, especially France and Belgium, were willing to intervene militarily to prop up authoritarian regimes or to defeat popular insurrections against arbitrary rule.

A further explanation of the erosion of democratic political norms may be found in the character of the post-colonial state. In the absence of a vigorous private sector, the state was perceived by political

---

1. Dependency theorists argued that their precarious economic situation was the outcome of a system of neo-colonialism which perpetuated under-development at the expense of national self-reliance and equitable growth (Brett, 1973; Leys, 1975).

leaders to be the prime source of personal enrichment and reward. This use of political power for private ends has been termed the 'extractive view of politics' by Hodder-Williams (1984:95-99). It helps to explain why politicians have been so reluctant to hand over power, and their willingness to use the control of government machinery to preserve their privileged access to the resources at its disposal. It also provides an insight into the reasons for state decay and economic decline in post-colonial Africa, which are explored in the next chapter.

2
The Growth and Decay of the Post-Colonial State

Over the past thirty years there has been a major shift in the way commentators have analysed the role of the state in Africa. In the early 1960s there was widespread agreement that the state ought to play a pivotal role in the post-independence period, both to promote rapid development and to provide the basis for a unified national identity. By the early 1980s there was a growing consensus in the literature that the state was no longer able to fulfil these objectives. The traditional emphasis on strengthening its interventionist powers in furthering political integration, engineering social transformation and promoting economic development has subsided. There is now a wholesale critique of the role of the state, within a general policy context defined by structural adjustment, privatisation and liberalisation (Doornbos, 1990). As a result, the African state is now increasingly identified with economic stagnation and as lacking in popular legitimacy.

The literature can be examined under three main headings: explanations for the expansion and consolidation of the post-colonial state; views on its role and principal functions; and interpretations of its growing malaise. Our point of departure is to consider briefly what 'the state' is commonly understood to mean in the political science literature and its application to the African situation.

The concept of the state

Although they differ in form, all modern states share four defining characteristics. These are: an association among people for the purpose of government; an organisation which has legally constituted sovereign status; an attachment to a particular territory; and a recognised entity in international law. The state is further identified with a particular set of institutions, which together constitute an apparatus of political authority and governmental power. These are the executive, the legislature, the bureaucracy, the judiciary, the police and the military. In theory, the executive and the legislature are expected to formulate and debate policy, the bureaucracy is responsible for the implementation of government policies and programmes, the judiciary interprets and applies public laws which are enforced by the police, and the military is responsible for defence and internal security. The officials who fill positions in these institutions themselves form an intrinsic part of the state apparatus, although it is debatable whether they represent a neutral or a vested set of interests. Viewed from this perspective, the classic definition offered by Weber, namely that the state is an organisation which monopolises legitimate force over a given territory, appears unduly restrictive since it presumes a fixed relationship between a territory and a political community; in much of Africa this very relationship is fluid and contestable.

Modern states also have a range of more specific functions associated with their role in the economy and the delivery of services which are undertaken by specialised agencies within the bureaucracy. The most important of these are their regulatory functions, where the objective is to create the conditions for balanced and sustained economic development. Modern states are also directly involved in production and investing in the economic and social infrastructure through public sector undertakings and social service provision. They also mediate between different classes and interest groups, most obviously between industry and labour. Clearly, these economic functions tend to be more pronounced in socialist regimes which are ideologically committed to a more expanded role for the state, although, as we shall see, the interventionist state has not been exclusively a feature of socialist regimes in Africa (Young, 1982).

The legacy of colonial rule

Differing explanations have been put forward to account for the specific characteristics of the post-colonial state in sub-Saharan Africa. Some commentators have emphasised the colonial inheritance, notably the political institutions developed under colonial rule and the mechanisms of revenue extraction created to maintain these. Young (1988) distinguishes three main phases of colonial rule, which may be summarised as follows (1988:41-56):

- **Construction of the colonial state**: hegemony was initially established by colonial conquest with the support of a network of collaborating intermediaries. This phase was typified by the construction of an apparatus of domination, with the revenue imperative (through fiscal measures and resource extraction) as the principal determinant of state construction.

- **Institutionalisation of the colonial state**: characterised by decentralisation and indirect rule, the perfection of institutions and the professionalisation of a cadre of administrators. 'Good government' became part of the legitimising fabric of the colonial state apparatus, with development and welfare constituting new elements in the colonial policy agenda.
- **Decolonisation**: the emphasis after the Second World War was increasingly on political reform, but not self-rule. There was a new concern with the creation of a political class of administrators which would rule within the framework of 'trusteeship'. This period saw the emergence of new doctrines of legitimation through regulated electoral contests. By the end of the colonial period sufficient institutional capacity had been accumulated to undertake significant development and welfare activities. Large-scale infrastructural investments and an expansion in health and educational services were made possible in the late 1950s by the post-war commodity boom which benefited African exports.

Although there were attempts to nurture an indigenous bureaucracy in the latter stages of colonial rule, senior administrative posts were still largely filled by European officials at the time of independence. In the majority of countries, the participation of Africans was for the most part restricted to clerical positions within the colonial administration (Jackson, 1986).

The political boundaries of most contemporary African nation-states also originated in the colonial era, when the imperial powers carved up the continent into zones of influence at the Berlin Conference of 1884-5. As noted in Chapter 1, these boundaries were closely attuned to the territorial ambitions of the competing European colonisers and tended to overlook ethnic and tribal affinities. Dunn observes that state structures were developed during the colonial period 'to subjugate from the outside and adapted primarily to represent external interests' (1986:164). This view stems from the notion of the 'over-developed' state, which argues that the state apparatus inherited at the time of independence was larger and had greater administrative and coercive powers than would have been the case if it had not been necessary to subjugate locally dominant classes (Leys, 1976).

The autocratic and hegemonic imperatives of the colonial state endured beyond independence and provided the organisational framework for its post-colonial successor. This statist legacy also found expression in extensive controls over trade and a dominant role for the public sector in infrastructural development which was to persist and deepen after independence.

Features of the post-colonial state

As outlined in Chapter 1, authoritarian personal rule rapidly became the hallmark of African states after independence, with military interventions becoming an endemic feature of post-colonial politics. At the same time, the size of the state itself expanded markedly, in terms of the numbers of functionaries, the coercive power of the security apparatus and the degree of intervention in the economy.

Young (1982) has observed that the growing prominence of the state in all spheres of life was not simply attributable to the ideological inclinations of those in power, although socialist regimes stressed the role of a dominant public sector as a bulwark against capitalism and foreign economic interests. Indeed, a commitment to 'statism' was shared by regimes of all political hues, for two main reasons. First, because after independence African leaders wanted to accelerate the pace of economic development and improve the welfare of their citizens through an expanded health and educational system, in part to satisfy the massive expectations aroused during the transfer of power. The second objective was increasingly one of self-preservation whereby rulers sought to maintain themselves in office at all cost. One way of doing this was to exploit the patronage networks which predated colonial rule, and enlarge the scope for sharing out the revenues and offices offered by the state.

The interventionist state

An emphasis on state intervention reflected a prevailing trend in development thinking which saw the state as the principal actor responsible for fostering economic growth in the drive towards self-sufficiency (Zolberg, 1968). A prominent role for the public sector was central to the ideology of Fabian socialism which imbued many nationalist movements in Asia and Africa. It was all the more compelling in African countries where an indigenous business class was either absent or primarily involved in export trade rather than manufacturing for the domestic market.

As noted earlier, the pre-eminent role of the state as an agent of economic transformation had already been established during the late colonial period (Young, 1988). After independence, there were four main elements to this. The first was the pressing need to build up the physical infrastructure through public investments in roads, railways, dams, power generation, utilities and telecommunications. The second was the development of a manufacturing and processing sector, largely through a strategy of import substitution, in order to encourage diversification and reduce the dependence of their economies on a narrow range of primary agricultural exports. Increased expenditure on social services, especially health and education, constituted the third major area of state intervention. The fourth was the formation of specialised bodies entrusted with the task of promoting rural development: agricultural extension services, rural credit agencies and departments responsible for managing natural resources.

African states also assumed a regulatory function, through the formulation and application of policies designed to govern the economy and to create the conditions for sustained economic growth and development. An array of fiscal measures (including deficit-financing) were employed to generate the resources necessary to fund these investments and recurrent expenditures, together with additional support in the form of external concessional finance. This revenue imperative primarily took the form of surplus extraction from agricultural producers, either as direct taxes on crop sales and excise duties or, more commonly, by keeping prices paid to farmers artificially low. The favoured mechanisms for this were state marketing boards, which for the most part were established under colonial rule (Bates, 1981).

A state class?

It has proved difficult to analyse the social character of African states using conventional class categories. Dunn (1986) argues that notions of national or comprador bourgeoisies are of little explanatory use in the African context since the ability of individuals to influence state power is not usually a function of their place in the socio-economic order. In general, the officials who inhabit the higher echelons of the state apparatus - career politicians, senior civil servants, the army officer elite, managers of public sector enterprises - also dominate political life. They tend to draw on a narrow social base, often with pronounced ethnic or regional biases, and constitute what Zolberg termed a 'bureaucratic gentry' (1966:142).

For these reasons the dominant class has been identified with a state class, where politicians and bureaucrats use state power to acquire capital and resources (Sklar, 1979). According to Young (1988:59): 'The ramifying state itself became the prime instrument of class formation, fostering the ascendancy of a political-administrative class whose own interests were tied to state expansion'. At the same time, this state class has tended to consolidate its dominance by acquiring a base of wealth outside the state, both to create the means for further accumulation and to guard against a possible loss of power and status following a change in regime (Diamond, 1987).

Azarya (1988) has shown that the state takes on multiple roles by virtue of the fact that it is composed both of institutions and of personnel who occupy offices and take decisions. At one level the state has been an autonomous actor in its own right, where it mediates between contending groups in the allocation of scarce resources; it is also an arena where different interest groups compete for scarce resources and attempt to gain influence over policy-making (see Chapters 4 and 5). Similarly Sandbrook (1986:68-72) argues that the state exercises a high degree of autonomy in decision-making and policy formulation, and serves as the prime locus for personal advancement and political power, since the indigenous capitalist class is generally weak in Africa.

At independence the departure of colonial officials offered opportunities for rapid advancement for those who had received training in the rules and procedures of the colonial administrative apparatus. The expansion of state economic activity in the post-independence period provided further opportunities for career progression. Yet the underdevelopment of the indigenous administrations weakened the effectiveness of African governments and fostered the growth of corruption in the absence of 'developed traditions and mechanisms of probity and responsibility' (Diamond, 1988a). Appointments were made on the basis of political influence rather than on merit and qualifications, as political leaders sought to spread the fruits of office among their constituents (Zolberg, 1968).

African bureaucracies are thus strikingly different from the Western norm of neutral administrations operating rationally on the basis of established rules and procedures. Indeed, this has led some commentators to question the very applicability of the notion of a bureaucracy in the African context. For example, Sandbrook argues that 'most African administrations diverge so widely from the model that the application of the term bureaucracy is quite misleading' (1986:325). Similarly Jackson and Rosberg (1988) suggest that the concept of the modern administrative state is of limited applicability in Africa because the state cadre is of questionable reliability and effectiveness.

The nature of state decay

In the 1980s, there has been a significant shift in the way that commentators view the role of the state, reflected in the fact that the state is no longer treated as the prime mover of development, but increasingly as its main constraint (Doornbos, 1990). This is in part due to changing perceptions among development practitioners and the ascendancy of neo-liberal economic thinking, but more importantly, it reflects the empirical reality of state decay in Africa, and the inability of many states to solve pressing economic problems. Although the institutional fabric of contemporary African states was largely shaped in the colonial period, it is increasingly clear that the decay that has taken place is closely related to the types of regimes that have predominated in the post-colonial era.

A common observation in the literature is that most African states exercise only a tenuous hold over the societies that they govern, giving rise to the notion of 'weak' or 'soft' states. Even though many African states (especially those characterised by autocratic personal rule) developed a powerful machinery to enforce control, they lacked legitimacy among the population, exhibited by the lack of popular support and tendencies towards secession or the emergence of a parallel economy (Azarya, 1988).[2]

The largely artificial political boundaries of most African states have in fact proved remarkably durable in the post-colonial period. None of the independent states have actually fragmented, and attempts to create larger political units have generally failed. Partly for this reason, Zolberg (1968) argued that political integration was very weak at independence and that the *de jure* existence of states did not necessarily imply full territorial control. African states were principally held together by the inertia characteristic of the colonial period and buttressed by the international political system.

Jackson and Rosberg (1988) maintain that many weak African states might well not have persisted without the recognition bestowed on them by the international community (official aid agencies, the Organisation of African Unity and other inter-governmental organisations). For this reason, they suggest that external rather than internal factors are more likely to provide an adequate explanation of

---

2. Drawing on the experience of Tanzania in the 1970s, Hyden (1983) argued that the state was too weak to prevent the peasantry from opting out of market incorporation (through regulated state marketing boards), which in turn reduced the ability of the state to extract a surplus. Others writing from a dependency perspective claimed that widespread incorporation had taken place but argued that adverse terms of trade and debt obligations limited the scope for alternative interventions on the part of the state (Doornbos, 1990).

their formation and persistence. These include the ideology of pan-Africanism, the support of the larger international community, and periodic intervention by external powers in the internal affairs of African states. Aid resources from international donors clearly played a role as well. In this respect they conclude (1988:22-3):

> International society is at least partly responsible for perpetuating the underdevelopment of the empirical state in Africa by providing resources to incompetent or corrupt governments without being permitted to ensure that these resources are effectively and properly used.

Three principal factors highlight the character of state decay in Africa today. The first and most obvious is the economic malaise that pervades most African countries, reflected in low or negative rates of development. Since the state has played a dominant role in African economies and has exercised significant autonomy in policy-making (see Chapter 4), it is thought to be at least partly responsible for this malaise, which has been exacerbated by drought, low resource endowments, heavy external debt and adverse terms of trade. The second is what Young (1988:26) terms the 'propensity to over-consumption' by the state, fuelled by unsustainable levels of public sector expenditure. The third factor is the growing disjuncture between the state and civil society, in which growing disillusionment with state performance has resulted in a process of disengagement, manifest in the growth of a parallel economy, withdrawal from the official markets smuggling capital flight, and migration (Azarya, 1988; Chazan, 1988). To these may be added in some cases a fourth factor, namely, the undermining of the state's capacity by tyrannical rule and protracted civil war, which have invariably resulted in institutional paralysis (Decalo, 1985).

Personal rule and patronage

Much of the blame for state weakness has been attributed to a tendency towards the 'patrimonialisation' of the state apparatus since independence ((Zolberg, 1966; Hyden, 1983; Sandbrook, 1985; Young, 1988). In Weber's definition, a patrimonial system is one in which the object of obedience is the personal authority of the individual ruler which he enjoys by virtue of traditional status and the loyalty of his subjects (Zolberg, 1966:140). According to Callaghy (1986), the patrimonial state in Africa has four essential features: a highly centralised executive authority is personalised around a presidential monarch or a military leader; charismatic, patrimonial and legal-rational doctrines are blended in an attempt to 'routinise' power;

personal rulers are supported by officials and new administrative cadres rooted in patron-client networks; and the state provides the major avenue of upward mobility, status, power and wealth.

Jackson and Rosberg (1982) have questioned the applicability of the concept of patrimonialism in post-colonial Africa since it presupposes that contemporary politics are founded on 'traditional' norms. They use the notion of personal rule in preference to that of patrimonialism on the grounds that there are no valid and operative political traditions which embody this form of rule at the territorial level. Rather, they argue that the very paucity of politically relevant traditions and the failure of rational procedures to become institutionalised are the reasons that rulership in Africa is so personalised. Similarly, Sandbrook (1986) accepts that patrimonial rule is associated with traditional authority, which has not remained the dominant form of rule in Africa (with the exception of the hereditary monarchies of Swaziland and Haile Selassie's Ethiopia). Like Jackson and Rosberg, he subscribes to the concept of personal rule, which he typifies as a form of patrimonialism characteristic of plural peasant societies.

Personal rule is rooted in patron-client relationships which provide the main form of societal articulation and the primary form of linkage between state and society (Jackson and Rosberg, 1982). These patron-client ties, for the most part based on ethnic and familial loyalties, are particularly strong and widespread in Africa and permeate African politics (Leonard, 1987).

There is a rich literature on patronage systems which cannot be thoroughly surveyed here, although two specific aspects are of interest to this review. First, there are the relationships of variants of patronage systems to competitive electoral politics. Second, there is the influence of patronage on economic policy formation and implementation, which is examined at some length in Chapter 4.

In a recent review, Lemarchand (1988) outlines a form of political patronage along the lines of the 'American machine' model in which support for the ruling elite/party is generated through the distribution of material incentives, usually in the form of public goods and services but also of jobs, rather than through appeal to ideology or principle. In the early years of independence the vote became a critical resource in the hands of citizens, to be traded for schools, piped water, scholarships and jobs. With the general decline of democratic politics since independence this patronage model survived mainly in Côte d'Ivoire, Kenya, Senegal, and Zimbabwe, or was confined to presidential elections in one-party states.[3]

Although in a sense patronage systems do represent a form of political accountability by bringing a range of ethnic and regional interests into the political process (Rothchild and Foley, 1988), these have centred on certain key elite groups, notably high-ranking officials in the civil service, the army and the police. Joseph (1983) has coined the term 'prebendalism' for forms of patronage primarily, but not exclusively, found in Nigerian politics, where power relations are more complex and dispersed. There is intense competition for 'prebendals' or offices which can be utilised for the personal benefit of the office-holder as well as that of their reference or support group, which in Nigeria is predominantly ethnically based.

For Joseph the underlying element in this system is clientelism, founded on an intricate and informal network of personal alliances which link communities in a pyramidal manner. Through these networks there is competition for state resources which reflects individual, communal and class motivations. Followers are rewarded with preferential loans, bribes, the illegal appropriation of private property and other forms of nepotism, all of which undermine bureaucratic authority (Sandbrook, 1986). This has assumed an exaggerated form in countries such as Zaire and Nigeria where politics are dominated by competition for access to public resources. Here the state becomes critical to material enhancement and state offices are used primarily for the benefit of patrons and clients (Joseph, 1983; MacGaffey, 1987).

Sandbrook (1985:112-144) argues that personal rule has undermined governance in a number of ways. First, it stultifies effective decision-making by eroding the independence of the bureaucracy and promoting the misallocation of scarce public resources. As a result, corruption and inefficiency have become systemic features of African bureaucracies. Under conditions of personal rule, bureaucratic accountability cannot be enforced in the absence of constitutional restraints or an influential business class. Secondly, the political requirements of regime and personal survival take precedence over and even contradict policies designed to promote sustained economic growth. Thirdly, personal rule fosters a climate in which decisions are taken on the

---

3. A careful assessment of a patron-client network and how it operated in Kenyan legislative elections is provided by Barkan (1984).

basis of short-term political considerations or for self-aggrandisement, with little regard to the longer-term consequences.

However, an excessive emphasis on the underlying causes of state decay as a universal phenomenon obscures the fact that there is considerable variation in the administrative capacities of African governments. As noted by Jackson and Rosberg (1988), there are striking differences between the relatively efficient administrations of Kenya and Côte d'Ivoire, and the swollen and ineffective bureaucracies found in countries like Mali, Togo and Congo. In states such as Zaire and Equatorial Guinea where the prime objective of public office is personal survival or self-aggrandisement, government structures hardly function at all (Sandbrook, 1986). One reason for this variation may well be the extent to which colonial rulers cultivated an indigenous administrative capacity (Young, 1988). A second factor is that in some countries, especially in Francophone West Africa and the former British colonies in southern Africa, the process of Africanisation was very gradual, with Europeans continuing to exercise an influential role in the civil service. Drawing on the experience of Côte d'Ivoire, Crook (1989) has questioned whether patrimonial rule is necessarily inconsistent with administrative autonomy, since President Houphouët-Boigny has insulated and protected a reasonably effective bureaucracy. This suggests that institutional safeguards and incentive systems may be as important as the political environment in determining administrative effectiveness.

Questions of administrative capacity lead us on to examine the process of economic policy-making more closely, and the influence of both state actors and interest groups respectively in shaping policy and policy outcomes. These form the subject of Chapters 4 and 5. The next chapter examines the various typologies of African political systems put forward in the literature, in order to tease out some of the distinctions between different types of authoritarian and personal rule that have until recently dominated the political landscape in Africa and which in turn may provide a basis for comparing economic policy performance.

3
Classifying African Political Systems

In order to comprehend the distinctive character of African politics better, a number of scholars have attempted to construct typologies for classifying and comparing different kinds of political systems. These entail a search for common structural features in the institutional make-up of the state, and the character of the regime, which form the basis for grouping together political systems into 'ideal-type' categories.[4] Typologies have also been used to analyse performance in terms of economic growth, social development, patterns of inequality, economic policy and adjustment (see Chapter 6).

It should be noted that while there are differences in emphasis between individual typologies, there is widespread agreement on the salient features of post-colonial African political regimes. Most have borne the stamp of personal rule, with political leaders playing a dominant role in the political process, either from an autocratic or a benign standpoint (Jackson and Rosberg, 1982). A second widely shared characteristic is their instability and ephemerality. Very few regimes have remained unchanged since achieving independence, with frequent alternations between civilian and military regimes (and various gradations within these) in many countries. Third, the state exerts a powerful influence over society whatever the ideological complexion of the individual regime, even though it may command little legitimacy (Lonsdale, 1981). The functions of party and state are often closely interwoven, especially in authoritarian and populist regimes. In what follows, various approaches to regime typologies are examined with a view to highlighting the insights that they offer in the African context. An alternative classificatory schema is also

---

4. Callaghy (1986:31) sounds a note of caution when he points out: 'The quest for sovereignty takes place within the context of poorly organised states with limited power resources which attempt to rule societies that are distinctly early modern internally and dependent externally. This general condition has continuously frustrated efforts to formulate grand, all-encompassing typologies of rule that productively differentiate between African states.'

outlined, which attempts to redress some of the limitations of existing typologies.

Personal rule and regime type

Jackson and Rosberg (1982:1) maintain that personal rule is the defining characteristic of African regimes:

> African politics are most often a personal or factional struggle to control the national government or to influence it: a struggle that is restrained by private and tacit agreements, prudential concerns, and personal ties and dependencies than by public rules and institutions.

This emphasis on the role of individual actors in the political process is based on the assumption that, in the absence of effective political institutions, personal rulers have played an important role in maintaining political order (Zolberg, 1968). As noted already, the overriding objective of personal rulers is to remain in power; this governs their actions and shapes the internal character of personalised regimes. Jackson and Rosberg (1982) see the key features of personal rule as follows:

- The absence of effective institutionalised rules and the establishment of a political game in which individuals and factions struggle for power and place and not one in which groups and parties compete for policies.
- Patron-client relationships between rulers and ruled in which support is achieved by financial rewards and access to power and privileged positions and is generally isolated from wider political processes and participation.
- Uncontested supremacy with personal rulers seldom subject to constitutional time limits on their incumbency, but enjoying unrivalled power, prestige, wealth and honour.
- Inherently authoritarian rule, monopolising power, eliminating constitutional checks and balances, centralising state power and limiting political rights (though not usually the right to possess private property or religious freedom).

Moreover, under such conditions, the head of state dominates political and cultural life. Strategic positions in the police, the military and the bureaucracy are filled by individuals loyal to him, especially close relatives and those attracted by the spoils of office, with a loyal armed force used to bolster personal rule when legitimacy is weak (Sandbrook, 1985).

On this basis Jackson and Rosberg (1982) identify four generic types of personal rule: princely, autocratic, prophetic and tyrannical. *Princely* and *autocratic rule* are both characterised by caution and conservatism in the use of state power, but they differ in their relations with elite groups. The Prince (such as Senghor of Senegal) rules jointly with other oligarchs to cultivate their loyalty, co-operation and support, and presides over preferential access to state resources, but prevents other leaders emerging as serious challengers. In contrast, the Autocrat (personified by Life-President Banda of Malawi) dominates the oligarchy and the state without having to share its resources with others. As Jackson and Rosberg observe (1982:78): 'Where the Prince presides and rules, the Autocrat commands and manages; the country is his estate ... '. In a manner reminiscent of the absolutist monarchies of Europe, the Autocrat wields complete discretionary power, but maintains a close identity with the populace, however contrived, in order to fend off potential rivals.

Prophetic rule is associated with political visionaries who set out to reshape societies in ways consistent with their ideology, which is usually grounded in populist socialism. Charisma is an essential trait of prophetic rule, which favours dirigiste policies for guiding state policy and cultivating the support of others. In this conception, Nkrumah or Nyerere are examples of the archetypal Prophet. When prophetic rule fails, usually through a lack of economic and political resources, disappointment and cynicism set in, and the political legitimacy of the regime is weakened, which makes it susceptible to overthrow. *Tyranny* is the most extreme version of personal rule; the dictatorial regimes of Amin, Nguema and Bokassa fall into this category, where repression and terror are used to enforce control. Such leaders exercise maximum power and resort to socio-economic patronage and outright plunder of state resources to reinforce their absolute dominance (Decalo, 1985).

While there are advantages in such an approach, in that it highlights the capacity of actors to influence historical events and political processes, Jackson and Rosberg's typology only considers regimes which display the stamp of personal rule, and leaves out other types of civilian and military regime which have ruled at different points in time in African countries. Although the categories that they use are descriptive, and not mutually exclusive or predictive, their basic contention that personal rule is the defining characteristic of most African regimes cannot be contested.

Existing classifications and their limitations

In order to overcome the limitations of a regime classification based on personal rule, Berg-Schlosser (1984) has put forward a broader categorisation. He distinguishes four types of political system which share common characteristics: polyarchy, socialist, authoritarian and military. The indicators that he uses are the degree of competitiveness in the party system, the pattern of recruitment of the executive, the basis of political legitimacy (electoral or traditional), the pattern of separation of power, namely vertical (independence of the judiciary from the executive) and horizontal (centralised or federal), the actual power structure (personalised or dispersed), the scope of political control, and the ideological orientation of the system.

Briefly, a *polyarchy* is defined as a regime where political leaders are responsive to the wishes of the people by means of free and fair elections, with freedom for opposition, a separation of powers with an independent judiciary, and the institutionalised rule of law. It is further premised on the existence of a participatory political culture and a relatively egalitarian social structure (Dahl, 1971). In the African context, where such conditions generally do not prevail, both semi-competitive and pluralist regimes are included within this category, which is offered in preference to the term democracy which Berg-Schlosser considers to be value-laden and too closely tied to Western political norms (1984:129-30).

Socialist regimes are associated with single-party structures, centralised government and an ideology which emphasises national self-reliance and an egalitarian social order. In such regimes both freedom of expression and pluralistic forms of organisation are curtailed. African socialist regimes (such as Tanzania) and Marxist-Leninist regimes (Angola, Ethiopia and Mozambique) are both included within this category, although these are distinguished from the former totalitarian regimes in Eastern Europe by virtue of their relatively underdeveloped condition and lack of effective social control.[5]

Authoritarian regimes are also characterised by single-party organisations, in which leadership is strongly centralised, and often highly personalised. There is no institutionalised competition for public office. There is little scope for expressing public opinion and the

---

5. For a distinction between these types of regimes, see Rosberg and Friedland (1964) and Young (1982).

media tend to be highly regulated. Such regimes enforce their legitimacy through repressive measures, although some rely on an element of popular support, usually for a charismatic leader. The class base of authoritarian regimes is narrow and they are ideologically inclined towards a capitalist market economy (Berg-Schlosser, 1984:130-1).

The fourth category employed by Berg-Schlosser are *military* regimes. Their salient features are a high degree of centralisation, often accompanied by marked personal rule, with a no-party system in which organised interests have limited influence. Ideologically, such regimes may display a preference for socialist-style centralised planning or for a market economy. Yet few military regimes retain these characteristics for any length of time. Some limit their role to handing over power to a popularly elected civilian regime. Where military leaders seek to institutionalise their rule they may opt for a single-party system, either with authoritarian features or follow the socialist model (Decalo, 1976). Military regimes which are unsuccessful in engineering such a transition or fail to establish a broader base of legitimacy are susceptible to being deposed by a rival armed group, often resulting in continued political instability. Such regimes, which Berg-Schlosser notes are the predominant type in sub-Saharan Africa, he terms *praetorian* (cf. Huntington, 1965).

The political dynamic encapsulated in the degree of regime stability gives rise to further sub-categories (e.g. stable polyarchic and stable socialist) which Berg-Schlosser uses as the basis for assessing various aspects of regime performance.

One problem with Berg-Schlosser's four-fold categorisation is that he mixes *ideological* characteristics (i.e. socialist) with forms of rule defined by their *institutional* characteristics (authoritarian, military and polyarchy). For example, authoritarian rule may also be associated with socialist regimes, even though he identifies it with regimes characterised by a capitalist orientation. A related problem lies with the use of the term 'polyarchy' in the context of African polities. Berg-Schlosser readily admits that it is more applicable to Western liberal democracy, especially since only nominally democratic regimes such as those in Kenya and Senegal are included under this category.

A second problem lies with the use of a residual category such as praetorian to classify regimes which display instability. Of the 38 countries examined by Berg-Schlosser, 22 are characterised as having praetorian regimes. This highlights an intrinsic methodological problem in attempts to construct regime typologies which have adequate explanatory power in the African context. This was especially true of the 1960s and early 1970s which were marked by chronic political instability.

In an attempt to overcome these types of limitations, Ravenhill (1980) has suggested three categories of regime: uninterrupted civilian rule, civilian regimes interspersed with military rule, and military regimes where government power was seized by force.[6] Yet from his review of regime performance, he questions whether military regimes are sufficiently distinct to warrant the construction of a separate generic category (p. 124):

> What is at issue here is whether there exists a 'political process' sufficiently distinct for all military regimes in Africa to enable generalisations to be made on an a priori basis. Such would not appear to be the case: rather there is a spectrum of political processes ranging from an open multi-party system to a dictatorship. Not all civilian regimes cluster at the 'open' end of the scale. Comparative political analysis requires an empirical determination of the characteristics of a particular regime, rather than assumptions based on the civilian/military dress of the head of state.

He further concludes (p.125): 'The ideal-type dichotomy between civilian and military regimes has not been fruitful for theoretical analysis; in contemporary Africa it only serves to obfuscate the heterogeneity of political processes and regime types'.

While much of what Ravenhill states is valid, it may nevertheless be possible to construct a regime typology which takes into account the problems of existing approaches, and at the same time avoids the dichotomy that he warns against. The basic problem of developing regime typologies with adequate explanatory power in the African context is that the majority have exhibited varying forms of authoritarianism. The challenge is to produce a classification that distinguishes convincingly between different types of authoritarian rule according to the nature of executive power and the commitment to civil and

---

6. A further category of 'mixed' regimes is employed for assessing the aggregate performance of all regimes subject to military rule, but it does not constitute a distinct regime 'type' (Ravenhill, 1980:106). Only 15 out of 45 African states retained their original system of government for at least ten years, which points to a basic problem involved in attempts to construct regime typologies, namely their tendency to go out of date relatively quickly unless they are continuously revised. This in turn complicates the task of generalising about regime type and performance over time, especially the task of disentangling regime character from instability in explaining performance.

political liberties. For the reasons discussed earlier, it is desirable to have a typology for the purpose of classifying regimes in sub-Saharan Africa which allows one both to generalise about regime characteristics, and if possible, to derive conclusions about their economic performance and policy outputs.

Besides the problems of classifying countries marked by regime instability and the limitations of ideological categories such as socialist, there is also a problem in identifying empirical characteristics on the basis of which meaningful distinctions can be made between different types of authoritarian regimes. As shown in Chapter 1, the dominant feature of post-colonial politics in sub-Saharan Africa has been authoritarian rule but authoritarian regimes range from the repressive tyranny of Amin's Uganda through to the benign autocracy of Banda's Malawi. Few countries have retained political systems that could be termed democratic, certainly for any significant period of time, which means that a simple authoritarian-democratic dichotomy is unlikely to prove particularly fruitful. Classifications grounded in a ranking of civil and political liberties also reveal little differentiation, since in practice most authoritarian regimes cluster around a very narrow band of indicators which are uniformly poor.

Although the use of military and authoritarian categories has been questioned on the basis that few meaningful differences in economic performance emerge, the typology presented in Figure 3.1 elaborates on the framework suggested by Berg-Schlosser with several modifications to his four basic (ideal-type) categories. The *military* and *authoritarian* categories are retained with some caveats, but the terms *populist* and *pluralist* are used in preference to socialist and polyarchical, bearing in mind the analytical limitations noted by Ravenhill (1980), since the framework employed here allows for differentiation between military regimes. The key characteristic of a military regime is not so much that it came to power in a takeover promulgated by army officers, but that the executive is controlled or dominated by military personnel and that there are no elections. Regimes which come to power by force but then institutionalise themselves through the formation of political parties and the appointment of civilian ministers are classed as authoritarian.

Populism is associated with regimes which seek to ground themselves in popular legitimacy by encouraging political participation, usually through mass organisations (trade unions, women's and youth associations, etc.) and sometimes through the ballot-box. Such regimes are party-based, generally to the exclusion of organised opposition groups (in the single-party form), and often highly personalised. They

Figure 3.1
Types and characteristics of African political systems

Type of Regime							
Ideal - type	*Sub-category*	*Party system*	*Electoral system*	*Political participation*	*Executive authority*	*Legislative autonomy*	*Judicial autonomy*
Military	Tyranny Dictatorship	No party	No elections	Exclusive	Personalised	None	Compliant
Authori-tarian	Leninist Autocracy Monarchy Oligarchy Guided democracy	Single party	Intra-party elections			Controlled	Limited
Populist	Social democracy Participatory democracy	One party dominance	Semi-competitive elections	Limited	Partly consultative	Limited	
Pluralist	Liberal democracy Polyarchy	Multi party	Competitive elections	Inclusive	Fully accountable	Substantial	Independent

tend to evoke self-reliance and favour an egalitarian social order, drawing on a rosy interpretation of pre-colonial history (as in African socialism) or the virtues of a shared African identity (pan-Africanism or negritude).

Pluralism refers to a form of rule which is premised on a distribution of political power among several institutions, with a diversity of associations in civil society which channel a multiplicity of concerns, values and interests to the state for deliberation and resolution. It is generally (but not necessarily) associated with competitive multi-party elections, a clear separation of powers, an independent judiciary and an active legislature which holds the executive accountable for its actions. Pluralism encourages a healthy respect for social and cultural diversity (traditional customs, religious and moral beliefs), political openness and the protection of civil liberties.

These four 'ideal-types' (pluralist, populist, authoritarian and military) can be further divided into a series of sub-categories (ranging from tyranny to polyarchy) which correspond to various combinations of regime characteristics. Eleven sub-categories are employed here mainly for illustrative purposes to show how regime types suggested in other typologies fit into this framework. At the top of the scale one finds various gradations of personal rule (Leninist regimes may be personalised or broader-based), and towards the bottom it may be appropriate to insert sub-categories akin to Sklar's democracy schema (1986).[7]

Six broad characteristics are used which draw substantially on those favoured by Berg-Schlosser and reflect the importance ascribed to them in other regime typologies. These are the party system, the

---

7. According to Sklar a liberal democracy is one in which the powers of government are limited by law and citizens enjoy freedom of association to compete for office in free elections at regular intervals. In this category he includes countries such as Nigeria (prior to the 1983 coup), Botswana, The Gambia, Mauritius, Senegal and Zimbabwe. In guided democracies (such as Kenya), the principle of accountability is retained but in the absence of multi-party electoral competition. The hallmark of social democracy (typical of Tanzania) is one in which the concept of democracy extends beyond the principle of accountability to the notion of social justice, with an emphasis on popular participation in pursuit of an egalitarian social order. Participatory democracy (for which he gives the example of Zambia) affirms the existence of a reciprocal relationship between democratic political and participative social institutions, with an emphasis on the educative effects of democratic participation in the workplace.

electoral system, the extent of political participation (a broader concept than elections), the nature of executive and legislative authority, the degree of judicial autonomy. The typology allows for overlaps in characteristics which may be shared by a number of different categories (and sub-categories) of regime. For instance, single-party systems may be associated with several types of regime: military, authoritarian, and populist. Similarly, one-party dominance, which may result from restrictions on opposition activity or from a powerful party which dominates all others, may feature in authoritarian, populist and pluralist regimes. The electoral system characteristic gives recognition to intra-party elections as well as to competitive multi-party elections. This is distinct from political participation which acknowledges that intra-party elections may preclude broad-based participation by restricting access to decision-making to a narrow party clique.

Although it is possible to find examples of regimes which fall outside these broad categories, or which do not correspond closely to the set of characteristics presented in Figure 3.1 (which could be expanded or modified), this typology does allow one to map out the successive regimes which have come to power in various countries in post-colonial Africa on the basis of these sub-categories, in order to give a deeper sense of the political dynamic. To illustrate the point, Ghana began its post-colonial political life with civilian rule under the Nkrumah regime in the 1957-66 period, which was then followed by a series of alternating military (1966-9, 1972-9, 1982-91) and civilian (1969-72, 1979-82) governments (Chazan, 1988). These civilian and military regimes spanned various sub-categories and displayed differing internal characteristics (the Nkrumah regime, for example, became gradually more authoritarian, with increasing restrictions on party activity and political participation, though it started out as a populist regime espousing African socialism).

The typology offered here enables one to relate discrete combinations of regime characteristics to past and present political regimes, and this both facilitates comparison and guides further exploration and interpretation of specific country experiences. However, this multiple classification may not permit statistically reliable correlation with economic performance, since there may be too few countries in each category. For such purposes (see Chapters 6 and 9), a ranking schema based on civil and political liberties may offer a more secure basis for comparison (Bollen, 1980; Gastil, 1987).

Part I
Summary and Conclusions

To sum up Part I, there is widespread agreement in the literature that the predominant characteristic of post-colonial politics in Africa has been personalised authoritarian rule with a prominent role for the military. This contrasts sharply with the liberal democratic constitutions that many states inherited at the time of independence and which represented a continuation of the habits set by colonial rule. The rise of authoritarianism has been explained by the persistence of ethnic divisions, weak political institutions, a shallow sense of nationhood, limited administrative and technical capacity, extreme economic dependence and unfulfilled popular expectations, all of which generated political insecurity and weakened the legitimacy of democratic regimes in the newly independent states. Single-party rule was institutionalised by means of constitutional changes and a gradual marginalisation of the political opposition through co-optation, harassment and patronage. Many countries experienced a series of military coups in which incumbent regimes were overthrown by force.

A mere handful of African countries have retained democratic or liberal democratic constitutions since achieving independence, among them Botswana and Mauritius. Both have small populations, are former British colonies and are seen by scholars as somewhat special cases. Their systems seem to reflect elements in the political 'culture'. In Botswana there is a similarity of language and cultural traditions in which no single ethnic group has dominated politics, and extensive consultation with traditional communal assemblies which has widened political participation. In Mauritius there is a common spoken language and official tolerance for minority languages, and a broad consensus over the desirability of multi-party democracy. There is also a willingness of different communities and interest groups to negotiate until a solution is found to economic problems. Political leaders are subject to intense public scrutiny, radical political activity has assumed constitutional forms, and there is widespread agreement over the concept of a mixed economy and the need to adjust policies to changing economic conditions. Good economic performance is seen as strengthening their democratic evolution as much as resulting from it.

The post-colonial state in Africa was in many ways modelled on the autocratic administrative traditions of the colonial state. Its size and influence grew markedly after independence, reflected in the number of people employed and the growth of a coercive apparatus. 'Statism' has been characteristic of both 'socialist' and 'capitalist' regimes in Africa where the state is associated with extensive intervention in the economy, restrictive controls over private sector activity, and a tendency to resort to the use of force to preserve national unity and territorial integrity. Contemporary African states are seen as unresponsive to the pressure of interest groups, unrepresentative of the wider society, and ineffective in the formulation and implementation of policy.

In many African countries, especially in those characterised by authoritarian personal rule, the state has become the major source of upward mobility, status, power and wealth, reflecting both the weakness of the private sector and scarcity of resources. Personal rulers are supported by an administrative class which preserves its power through patronage networks in which supporters are rewarded for their loyalty in the form of jobs and resources. This has given rise to a system of 'clientelism' which is founded on an informal network of alliances based on ethnic, familial and personal loyalties, in which politics is dominated by competition for access to public resources. Much blame has been placed on this system for ineffective policy formation and poor public sector management.

Yet despite the growth of the state it has been argued that many African states are essentially 'weak' states since they do not command legitimacy in the eyes of the population and their authority does not extend in equal measure throughout the territory under their nominal control. This has resulted in a wholesale disengagement from formal state structures, with the growth of a significant parallel market in many countries, withdrawal from state marketing corporations on the part of the peasantry, and widespread migration.

There has been a perceptible shift in the literature since the 1960s, when the state was treated as the principal agent of economic development, to a situation in the 1980s when the state was seen as the main obstacle to progress. Africa's economic decline is now attributed more to internal political factors than to external influences.

There have been a number of different attempts to classify African political regimes which centre on characteristics such as the party system, elections, political participation, the nature of collective authority, the role of legislatures, and the degree of autonomy in the exercise of political power. Other classifications have focused on ideological and civilian/military distinctions.

The literature suggests that a four-fold classification - military, authoritarian, populist and pluralist - may be appropriate. Under military and authoritarian regimes there is either no functioning party system or a single-party system predominates; elections are either absent or restricted to inter-party competition; there is no provision for popular participation; there is a strongly centralised executive; the legislative assemblies are either weak or completely absent; the judiciary exercises limited autonomy; and the scope of political control is highly repressive. Populist and pluralist regimes (the latter are rare in the African context, at least until recently) range from one-party dominance through to a multi-party competitive system with regular elections; political participation is encouraged, the executive is more accountable and the legislature tends to play a more active role; the judiciary has greater autonomy and is independent of the executive, and there is provision for free and open political debate.

The challenge is one of finding meaningful empirical distinctions among various types of authoritarian regimes. These constitute the largest single category of regime type in sub-Saharan Africa, but exhibit clear differences in terms of their commitment to civil and political liberties, their internal institutional arrangements, and the basis of compliance, which may be reflected in patterns of policy-making and performance. Part II examines the basis of this putative relationship in order to tease out the principal political influences on policy formulation in African states.

Part II

Sub-Saharan Africa: The Politics of Economic Policy Formation

4
State, Party and Parliament in Economic Policy-Making

The extensive decline in economic (and sometimes social) performance in Africa between the 1970s and the mid-1980s has been well documented. As well as changes in political culture, political institutions and types of regime, economic and political decline have been linked. The present study provides an analytical and empirical background for assessing recent suggestions that liberalisation of the political culture and institutions of sub-Saharan Africa with a shift towards more 'open', 'accountable' politics and a more pluralist society, would help reverse the political decline and contribute towards economic success (Hurd, 1990).

Part II is concerned with (a) political explanations of the economic policy agendas, choices and patterns and their implementation in sub-Saharan Africa in the 1960s and 1970s and (b) how major policy change and reversal in the 1980s in certain African countries has been explained. In Chapter 9 we speculate on the proposition that more 'representative' government in Africa will mean more effective economic governance.

Policy patterns and processes in Africa: the 1970s

There was a fairly common pattern to African economic policy in the 1970s and early 1980s which included the following recurring features: the persistence of high and volatile public sector deficits, often financed from the banking system; failure to stabilise inflation, especially in the face of terms-of-trade shocks; lack of clear prioritisation of public expenditure and weak economic appraisal of investment together with overvalued exchange rates, low prices (particularly for agricultural producers), excessive input subsidies and excessive protection for manufacturing. In addition, monopolistic and inefficient public marketing institutions, the development of other inefficient and uncompetitive parastatal bodies, the poor standard of public sector services and weak financial policies ('financial repression'); these and others frequently emerge from the literature on African economic and political decline. During the 1980s some of these policy trends began to be reversed in a number of countries. The reforms and changes are surveyed and evaluated in a series of WIDER and World Bank studies (Taylor, 1987; World Bank, 1988a, 1988b, 1989a, 1989b, 1990b; Mosley *et al.*, 1991).

Although political scientists differ in their interpretations, they seem to perceive three stages in the policy process: (i) *agenda setting* i.e. how do issues get on to the policy agenda?, (ii) the criteria and influences which determine the *formulation* or content of policy, and (iii) the *implementation* of policy, which can mean introducing and sustaining new policies or operating the policy where this requires continuing administration (Grindle and Thomas, 1990).

Following Killick (1989:chapters 3-5), good governance in relation to policy *formulation* suggests the setting of: (i) clear strategic choices (an open or closed economy, the balance between state and markets, etc.); (ii) clear policy objectives or targets and policy instruments to pursue them; (iii) criteria for choosing between policy instruments (i.e. magnitude of response, speed, and probability of effect, acting directly on the problem, their resource costs and flexibility). Also there is the likely public reaction and hence credibility, and the width and depth of impact on societal groups (the gainers and losers); and (iv) the need for consistency in the system of instruments used and the appropriate sequencing. For sustainable and effective *implementation* there are conditions which need to be satisfied if the intention of the measures is not to be thwarted by (a) those whose interests are threatened by it and (b) those who are simply unable to cope with informational and administrative demands (e.g. reduced controls of credit which limit scope for favouritism in allocation, or expenditure taxes that are too complicated to be enforced properly, etc.). Overall, Killick suggests that formulation and decision should be governed by simplicity; by available or planned administrative capacity; by identification of responsibility and awareness of interests; and by the motives of those involved in implementation. Sustainability probably depends most on correctly anticipating the likely public and political impact.

The following observations drawn from the critical literature and from those with personal experience, provide an insight into what has frequently happened in African governments, particularly during the 1970s (see Hyden, 1983; Armstrong, 1986; Gulhati, 1989, 1990; Grindle and Thomas, 1990; Callaghy, 1990).

Agenda setting

- The political agenda has been too narrow and determined centrally by executive and party with limited public debate and often limited debate among the top political leadership.
- There has been delay and indecisiveness in changing the economic policy agenda in the face of deteriorating conditions; also ineffective policies and growth of parallel economies.
- Reform agendas have not been drawn up in a timely way and hence decisions have often been made in 'crisis' situations.

Policy formulation

- Policy-making has been confined to very narrow policy circles and there has been little prior consultation with those likely to be affected by the policies. There has been limited dialogue with private interests and usually limited information available to policy-makers on the interests of particular societal groups.
- With some exceptions, there has been little attempt to seek a wide political consensus on the policies. Consultation on policy decisions has sometimes been viewed as 'a weakness'.
- There has sometimes been a dearth of decision-making. Major policy decisions are often the composite of many relatively minor decisions and if these are not made then meaningful policy does not evolve.
- The objectives of policies (e.g. on exchange rates, foreign-exchange allocations, parastatal management) have seldom been clearly articulated.
- In some countries, unrealistically ambitious plans have been pursued, given the resource availability and feasible delivery, instead of an 'incremental' approach to change.
- Plans commonly have not had adequate prioritisation and sequencing or adequate definition of executive responsibility with little co-ordination or interaction between bureaucratic departments after the decisions have been taken.
- There has been a tendency towards 'short-termism' in policy thinking and action.
- There has been a lack of demand by those in power for rational data collection, policy analysis, financial management and planning. Hence there have been technical weaknesses in the presentation of options to the political leadership. On the supply side, partly because of lack of skills, there has been lack of information, prior diagnosis and analysis of policy options before

decisions were taken. There have been weak links with universities and other independent domestic expertise.

- There has been lack of independence and autonomy on the part of administrators/advisers in putting forward proposals to the leadership and often failure to ensure rapid feedback to the political leadership on the outcome of policies in operation in order to guide a mid-term change of course.
- Policy formulation and the roles of the public service, parastatals/private sector or the size and structure of the civil service have not been seen as priority issues in the reform of the bureaucracy.

Policy implementation

Policy reform was often decided without simultaneous consideration of how it would be implemented. Donors have abetted this lack of co-ordination by agreeing policy changes and not always checking compliance. The dominant concern of observers has been with low system productivity combined with a style of management which was averse to risk and responsibility. Policies and their intentions were often changed, modified or evaded during the process of implementation so that the outcome was different from what the decision-takers intended.

Weak management systems, overstaffing, poor incentives, low pay and morale, poor skills, made implementation of objectives (e.g. by public enterprises and parastatals) slow and difficult.

Announced policy changes were often sudden, unexpected and lacked credibility with the public, hence undermining their influence and effective implementation, especially when they were sometimes reversed.

The literature and approaches

Despite a large literature on both economic policy and performance (largely written by economists) and politics and political change (largely written by political scientists, sociologists and historians), the literature which carefully and closely links the two is much smaller and more diffuse. This literature falls into several categories. First, general political studies which analyse the nature of the state, the character of political institutions and political culture in Africa since independence, and which seek to explain the state's systemic influence on public policy-making, public administration, and economic and social outcomes (e.g. Bates, 1981; Hyden, 1983; Sandbrook, 1985; Gulhati, 1991). Second, a large number of political economy studies of particular countries or regions (e.g. Chazan, 1986; Holm, 1986; Rimmer, 1986; Pryor, 1991). Third, case studies and comparative work on adjustment policy experience especially in the 1980s (e.g. Callaghy, 1990; Grindle and Thomas, 1989, 1990; Mosley *et al.*, 1991). Fourth, studies of specific aspects of public sector management and public administration (eg. Leonard, 1987).

Our approach explores the literature for insights into African political experience and distinguishes and assesses the motives, organisation and influence of the different 'actors' in economic policy. We distinguish four main influences on the formation of policy:

- **The state**: the executive, including the role of the political leadership, the bureaucracy and its relations with the political rulers, and other predisposing influences on state elites, such as ideology. The main question is how far economic policy is determined 'autonomously' by the state, what features of the state apparatus or regime 'explain' the character of policy choice and what constraints have operated on state action.
- The **legislature** and **party** systems: the role and influence of the legislature, individual Mps, single party and multi-party influence where it exists or has existed. What role has the 'separation of powers and checks and balances' through party and legislature played in influencing or constraining policy action by the state executive?
- **Civil society**: organised domestic interest groups and the scope for them to influence policy and policy change.
- **External financial agencies** and their influence both over time and relative to domestic forces.

The assessment focuses first on the pattern of policy in the 1970s and early 1980s and then on factors inducing major policy change in the 1980s. In ordering scholarly perceptions in this way we pick up a range of approaches to policy change in recent political work which has been usefully classified by Grindle and Thomas (1989) into the following categories:

- **'State-centred'** approaches which argue that the perceptions and interactions of policy elites and the broad orientations of the state more generally account for policy choices and their subsequent pursuit. This perspective views the state as analytically separable from society and the state elites as having interests which they adopt and pursue with some autonomy. These interests include the pursuit of ideologies of 'national interest' or the achievement and maintenance of the state elite's own hegemony vis-à-vis societal actors and the particular self-interests of regime incumbents.

- **'Society-centred'** approaches which explain or predict policy choice in terms of the values, perceptions, behaviour and historical or international contexts of social classes and interest groups. These encompass neo-Marxist theories for which social class formation and changes in the composition of the dominant class or class allegiance are the key to policy formation and political change, and pluralist perspectives which see the state as a neutral arbitrator among competing organised interests in society where its principal role is to respond to societal pressures and changes in the balance of these pressures. Public policy results from conflict, bargaining and coalition formation among potentially large numbers of societal groups organised to advance the interests of their members. There is little or no literature on how African governments consult interest groups in formulating policy.
- **'Public choice'** models of policy determination. These share basic assumptions with pluralist thinking but view both societal interest groups and elected (and non-elected) government officials as purely self-interested, with the latter predominantly concerned to maintain power by attracting and rewarding supporters and favouring certain groups. 'Rent-seeking' via policy formation and implementation is a major feature of this process. This school sees the outcome of these competing interest groups as unfavourable to the collective interest. 'Rational' politics in its view generates irrational economic policies. This school might be placed in either the state-centred or society-centred category, since it involves both.[8]

The political literature tends to be anecdotal rather than systematic in its assessment of policy; it also lacks careful time-profiles of policy change in specific countries in response to economic stagnation, political influences and crises. There are few systematic comparisons of country differences in both policy pattern and policy change. Some

---

8. The literature on 'public choice' and 'rent-seeking' is now large. See Collander (1984); Srinivasan (1985). The most well known application to Africa is Bates (1981), but see also Findlay (1989). Recent reviews and critiques are Grindle (1989); Toye (1990); Skalnes (1989); Herbst (1989).

exceptions (Young, 1982; Berg-Schlosser, 1984; 1989; Pryor, 1991) are reviewed below. There tends to be some discontinuity in the literature between writing which attempts to 'explain' the 1970s policy syndrome and economic decline and that which looks at the politics of adjustment and the 'responsiveness' of state policy in the 1980s.

The prevailing scholarly assessment of economic policy in Africa is rather 'static' and hence pessimistic up to the mid or late 1980s. Since then the literature on economic policy change has become more 'dynamic', looking at the domestic and external forces and the specific contexts and types of political regime which may have influenced policy reform or the lack of it. There is little writing, as yet, on the 'ideological' changes which may be taking place in some African societies.

State-centred perspectives

The rest of this chapter reviews 'state-centred' interpretations of economic policy. 'Society-centred' approaches are dealt with in Chapter 5.

Political leadership: personal and patrimonial rule

The motives, character and style of rule of political leaders clearly have an important influence on economic policy-making and implementation. Some scholars place the *main* responsibility for economic decline on the distinctive character of political systems in Africa, namely personal rule and patrimonial politics.

The key features of personal and patrimonial rule which bear on policy were outlined in Chapter 2. Briefly, they were the absence of effective institutionalised rules and political competition and rulers who relate to the ruled (or some of them) by patron-client relations, isolated from wider political processes within participation achieved by financial rewards and access to power and privileged positions. Personal rulers are seldom subject to constitutional time limits on their incumbency and are inherently authoritarian in monopolising power and eliminating constitutional checks and balances.

Our interest is in how these dimensions of political rule are likely to influence economic policy-making and policy implementation. Jackson and Rosberg (1982:18) see personal rule in Africa as:

> systems to regulate power in the state ... or carry out political functions (such as stability) but they are not systems of public governance or of 'rationalist' decision making ... nor a system in which the ruler aims at policy goals and steers the government apparatus by information 'feedback' and learning. Governance is more a matter of seamanship and

less one of navigation; that is staying afloat rather than going somewhere.

They note that success or failure in policy is unlikely to bring direct political rewards or losses; authoritarian governments cannot be displaced (in competitive elections) for their policy failures because of a lack of accountability, hence the reduced importance of the wider external environment on policy choice. Sandbrook (1988:321) similarly asserts:

> Political requirements of regime and personal survival take precedence over and can contradict the economic policies and practices needed to promote sustained expansion.

A number of other political scientists consider the ideological aspirations and personal characteristics of the national leader to be important determinants of government policies (e.g. Cartwright, 1983; Kirk Greene, 1991).

More specific influences by which personal rule is seen to impact adversely on policy include the following:

- Extreme uncertainty about any policy change or its durability (Jackson and Rosberg, 1982:30).
- Unpredictability, abruptness and idiosyncrasy of policy (Decalo, 1985; Zolberg, 1966:190). Administrative staff do not consist of officials, but personal retainers. 'What determined the relations of the administrative staff to the chief is not the impersonal obligations of office, but personal loyalty to the chief.' (Zolberg, 1966:190).
- A small, closed policy-making circle (Armstrong, 1986; Gulhati, 1990).
- Personal idiosyncrasy. '[T]he more autocratic the system of rule, the more likely is policy to be determined by the ruler and therefore the more subject it is to a change in direction.' (Jackson and Rosberg, 1982:30). However, it has been quite possible for a patrimonial leader to adopt a rational system of administration with technically specialised officials.

Some case studies on Africa bring out more specific aspects of personal rule on policy-making. The autocratic style of personal rule in *Malawi* (see Gulhati, 1989a; Pryor, 1990) generated a bureaucracy which tended to be reactive and obedient. Policy ideas in circulation were likely to be those which President Banda wanted and fear of dismissal weakened capacity for, and competition between, ideas. Willing to delegate much detailed oversight of the economy to technocrats, the President's interests focused on key political/economic issues such as opposition to socialist ideology, prices and fiscal balance (Kydd, 1988). However a great weakness was that advisers were afraid to remit bad news to higher authority and there was delay in delivering adverse 'feedback' on how policy was working. This sometimes delayed or prevented mid-course correction of policy and hence weakened the flexibility and adaptability of the policy process (Gulhati, 1989).

Although the President used the parliament and party to rubber stamp decisions rather than to debate and discuss them, there is evidence that 'outsiders' were used to float new policy ideas to him - and not just those representing the international financial institutions. And he has taken soundings within the party on grassroots grievances which must have included reactions to his policies even though the national policies were not debated. He is thought to take account of the diverse interests of different regional groups as well as of the larger farmers.

The paradox of the Malawi case is that, despite these weaknesses of the personalistic, autocratic presidential style, Malawi's record on economic policy and indeed economic performance has been one of the best in Africa, considering its initial inheritance (Pryor, 1991). At the same time, its record on social development rates as one of the worst in Africa, reflecting the relatively low priority given to expenditure on health and education.

Zambia provides an example of another autocratic president, Kenneth Kaunda. Policy-making under Kaunda was highly centralised, ultimately bypassing the cabinet and the bureaucracy and centralising party power in the hands of the President. Policy was not significantly based on any technical analysis. Lack of consensus (which could not be achieved by patrimonial means) undermined implementation. Economic policy was a failure over long periods - as shown in an inability to control budgets, establish an effective wage policy, execute appropriate price and exchange-rate changes, etc. It was delayed and indecisive at vital points, and despite the similarity in style of personal rule, the economic outcome was much less satisfactory than in Malawi, given the differences in national endowments of the two economies (Gulhati, 1989b).

In a study of *Tanzania* and its government, van Donge and Liviga (1986) express reservations about explanations that stress personal rule. They emphasise the 'political culture' which stresses consensus and aversion to risk-taking. A strong 'visionary' president was surrounded by a political elite, which displayed unity and conformity, not because of coercion or purges, but because of a wish to avoid conflict and division (1986:637-8).

> Policy making appears to be in the hands of the President surrounded by a small group of people who tend not to be Cabinet Ministers .... There must be opportunities for independent policy making by individual Ministers in Tanzania because stability ... allowed some Cabinet Ministers to stay in power for long periods ... and build strong power bases. That they did not, reflected on themselves not on heavy controls by the President.

For the economic drift and decline of *Sierra Leone*, Lukes and Riley (1989) place considerable responsibility on personal rule and the lack of will and skill on the part of the leadership to secure the compliance of the more powerful supporters of the regime by means of necessary policy changes which were not in their short-run interest. However, they believe that personal rule is not inconsistent with successful economic management, provided the style and ideology are appropriate and the administration is insulated from the worst effects of this type of governance - as in Malawi, Côte d'Ivoire and Cameroon.

Decalo (1985) explores the personalistic 'tyrannical' dictatorship in which all policy dictates derive from an absolute ruler and all society is viewed as his personal fief, whether social or political structures are *pro forma* retained or not. Almost by definition, it may not be possible to generalise about 'personal' authoritarian types of policy and economic performance. Diamond, Linz and Lipset (1988:18) in their major study of African democracy say:

> Our evidence on performance, both political and economic, repeatedly calls attention to the importance of political leadership. The values and skills of political leaders have figured prominently in the destruction or nurturance of democracy .... They (the leaders) have displayed an intolerance of criticism and a distaste for consultation and compromise ....

It is currently contended that open debate of policy, consultation with interested parties, compromise with various interest groups and a search for consensus are most likely to ensure that economic policy formation is workable, acceptable and sustainable (World Bank, 1989b:193). This may seem plausible but, as Killick (1989:46) has pointed out, it is also an untested hypothesis. Indeed, perhaps because there has been so little 'consultation' and 'compromise' in sub-Saharan Africa, there are very few studies on how they work and affect policy processes. (Botswana's 'consensus' policy-making is considered below.)

The role of ideology

The independent power of ideas and changes in ideas is probably underrated in scholarly research. Ideas and their influences are rather intangible and it is difficult to trace and measure their source and movement. However, considerable work has been done on ideology in Africa, its substance and its effects on economic performance. Rather less has been done on how far the ideology of the leaders or state elites influences their policies and even less on how these ideologies change.

Crawford Young (1981), in a systematic review of ideology and development in Africa since independence, classified states into three categories: (a) capitalist, (b) populist socialist and (c) Afro-Marxist. While accepting the 'dependence' of most African economies and that political or economic imperatives forced upon regimes choices that appeared inconsistent with their ideological preferences, Young nevertheless concluded that ideology *mattered* in their actions. His study explored differences in the approach to policy-making and rather more thoroughly the systematic association of ideological differences with outcomes in terms of economic growth, equality, civil rights and other aspects of their performance.

The '*capitalist*' ideology category (seen as fitting Kenya, Côte d'Ivoire, Nigeria and perhaps Malawi) was associated with policies which gave importance to the private sector and private ownership of property, and openness to international trade and foreign capital. The '*populist socialist*' ideology of states like Tanzania, Ghana, and Guinea Bissau in the 1970s conditioned their policy choices to encourage a large public sector and a statist approach to development, radical rural reform and concern for the rural peasantry. The '*Afro-Marxist*' group of countries, encompassing Madagascar, Mozambique, Ethiopia, etc., chose a non-capitalist path with large-scale nationalisation, extensive parastatal sectors and bureaucracies, and state involvement over the whole productive sector. Overall, Young concluded that ideological preferences did influence the matrix of policies, and that their cumulative effect over two decades (1960s and 1970s) differentiated the three groups, but that neither economic growth nor equality outcomes were systematically related to ideological inclinations.

Two recent paired comparisons also bring out distinct policy patterns which correlate with different ideology and value systems: Pryor (1990) in a comparison of Madagascar and Malawi, and Berg-Schlosser (1989) on Tanzania and Kenya. However, Ake (1984) in a comparison of the latter 'pair' takes a sceptical view of the influence of ideology. He sees it as a response to changing objective conditions (e.g. terms of trade, aid flows) and believes that, after their divergence since independence, these two countries will converge in their ideological character.

During the 1980s more indicators of economic policy positions and intermediate economic variables emerged as a result of World Bank research work. These appear to show some association with Young's ideological groupings. Domestic savings rates in the 1980s were distinctly and consistently higher in the 'capitalist' countries and the worst performers were the Afro-Marxist states, confirming Young's judgment in 1981 that 'no Marxist regime has yet achieved forced draft economic expansion'.

Trade policy orientation - whether outward or inward looking - for the period 1975-85, as evaluated by the World Bank (1987) seems also to be closely correlated with these ideological groups, except for Nigeria. There is also the (expected) tendency for measures of domestic price distortions to be lower in the capitalist category and highest in the socialist countries - Nigeria again being the exception. On the other hand, the scale of the public sector as measured by the ratio of public expenditure to GDP, seems to have increased steadily and systematically across all African countries over the last two decades without regard to ideology; 'statism' has been a common feature. In Zimbabwe, Herbst (1989) sees the growth of the public sector as due to patronage and concern about foreign ownership rather than to socialist ideology *per se*.

There has been no major comparative study of ideology or policy patterns of African countries since Young's work. The extent to which ideology may be *changing* in Africa in accordance with substantial changes in policies in the 1980s has not yet been fully assessed by scholars.

Clientelism and policy formation

Patronage and clientelism as a feature of Africa politics was reviewed in Chapter 2. A number of studies place a strong responsibility on patron-client systems for the economic ills that Africa has faced. They are seen as a major influence on the *pattern of policy* in the following studies on African political economy: Bates, 1981; Hyden, 1983; Leonard, 1987; Barkan, 1984; Sandbrook, 1985; Herbst, 1989, 1990; Lemarchand, 1988; Gulhati, 1990.

The adverse implication of this type of clientelism for economic policy formation is universally asserted but the special spheres, the process of its influence and its relative importance are less clearly spelt out. The following processes can be identified, although it is not always easy to separate influence via formal policy design from implementation and action by state officials.

First, the development of patron-client linkages places a strong emphasis on the 'distribution' of state resources to those supporting the party or regime, at the expense of wealth-creation. Both Joseph (1983) for Nigeria and Barkan (1984) for Kenya see these features of the electoral process as ambiguous and self-destructive. Thus Barkan (1984:29-30) says for Kenya;

> with each successive election more and more communities become more effectively linked to their government via a network of patron-client hierarchies or machines ... [by which] those at the periphery gain access to those at the top ... as more and more communities make effective demands on the centre the amount of resources available for allocation to each community will be reduced and the intensity of political conflict ... will increase ...

Shams (1989:77) more recently describes the importance of clientelist systems on policy in Kenya as follows:

> The ethnically biased clientelist system is not, however, allowed to jeopardise the security of the state: political affairs are conducted by factions and cliques, who mediate between the leadership and ethnic, regional and sectoral interests and contend with one another for control over resources. Under these conditions, the allocation of political offices, investment flows and the prices for important goods and services are politically regulated. Changes incite the opposition of those affected and everything is done to avoid any disturbance in the delicate balance of interests which could rock the political boat. Only for political reasons, i.e. only when major battles within the various strategic groups or subfactions are waged, are changes made in the mode of distribution and hence existing regulations. Under these circumstances, adjustment measures aiming at economic rationality can easily clash with the political rationality of the system. Only those components of an adjustment programme have a chance of being implemented which do not run counter to the politically predetermined distribution structure.

Joseph (1983) takes a similar view for Nigeria where the centralisation of massive but unstable oil revenues has encouraged this syndrome. He sees patrimonialism/prebendalism as operating under both military and civil regimes, but believes it flourishes and is *worse* in periods of multi-party elections. The Nigerian Constitution of 1979 made the informal norm of political competition, that all government appointments and disbursements reflect the federal character, into a directive principle of state policy.

> With the return to competitive party politics after 1978 constraints to the full flowering of prebendal politics were removed. The winning of elections calls for heavy financial investment by aspirant candidates and their parties in Nigeria and the recouping of such investments cannot be done without the simultaneous distribution of public resources to sectional constituencies.

Joseph believes this placed heavy pressure on state budgets and created indebtedness and he also maintains that those who gained office were able to block, alter or circumvent state policies to suit their own needs.

Callaghy (1986) also sees a deep crisis or contradiction under patrimonial politics, which is not going to be relieved by policy initiatives or changes of regime. Thus, those who achieve public positions are violently assailed for abuse of office while simultaneously being prevailed upon to preserve some benefits for their artificially expanded networks of sectional supporters. What is more, there is a very high premium on keeping power, which means that divisions go deep in politics and make a democratic ethos 'fragile'.

Effects on specific policy areas

One contention is that government revenues are diverted away from development or investment uses towards recurrent expenditures with lower returns. However, this needs to be established more rigorously not least because much of the ethnic/regional pressures have been for expenditures on schools, health facilities, water supplies, rural roads - most of which are currently viewed as having high if delayed social returns. Of course, reduction of non-wage recurrent resources has had an adverse effect in a number of African economies.

Second, in public investment allocation, the desired political influence over the location, nature and priorities of public sector projects - driven by ethnic, territorial and other favoured constituencies - has probably thwarted the use of more rigorous economic appraisal criteria.

Third, the excessive politicisation of social life not only creates expectations which cannot be fulfilled by the state but gives the wrong signals to the potential indigenous independent entrepreneurs, and encourages lazy, rent-seeking 'drone' capitalists.

Fourth, a cumulative growth of the state - in terms of resource claims and ownership - has been encouraged by this process. It has also been a factor in government's growing parastatal sectors and budgetary deficits in the 1970s and 1980s (e.g. for Zimbabwe, see

Herbst, 1989). Decentralisation in the public sector has been discouraged in Kenya for these reasons (Grindle and Thomas, 1989).

Fifth, in order to operate patron-client systems and keep access to the political arena in check, politicians and officials have extended political control over a wide area of economic activity and rewards (Hyden, 1983). This has encouraged *direct* political control over the allocation of not only public but also private resources and has allowed individual discretion which permits targeting of rewards for specific support groups. In the view of Gulhati (1990) this has biased governments against impersonal 'market-oriented' policy.

Policies in respect of money and credit, foreign exchange, import and investment licences are examples. Thus, in the financial sector, credit allocation by banks and parastatals has not generally been determined by interest rates, creditworthiness and financial viability criteria but by direct administrative and often political intervention. See for example, Lane, (1989:18-19) for Côte d'Ivoire and the West African Monetary Union, and Killick and Mwega (1990) for Kenya. General policies of 'financial repression' - low and negative real interest rates and direct credit controls - have undoubtedly been resistant to change because of the individual political discretion which clientelism encourages. High percentages of 'non-performing' bank credits are an indicator of the adverse effects. Estimates of the economic penalty of these policies have been reviewed by Gelb (1989).[9]

Sixth, agricultural policies have been biased against rural interests as a result of clientelism, according to some scholars. Lemarchand (1988), for example, claims that patronage has had a negative effect on rural producers. He seems to base this perception largely on the Bates (1981) thesis that rural producers - especially peasant smallholders - were exploited by low procurement prices and large margins in parastatal marketing systems intended to increase the volume of patronage resources at the centre as well as by the inefficiency and personal corruption in these institutions. Lemarchand attributes a significant responsibility to patronage for the development of parallel markets in sub-Saharan Africa.

Thus the political literature suggests that patronage has had a direct effect on African economies via the implementation (or mis-imple-

---

9. He suggests (with caveats) that low real interest rates are directly related to the efficiency of investment and that measures of 'financial depth' 'explain' some variation in growth rates, in cross-country comparisons.

mentation) of policies as well as their formulation, but it also indicates that major policy change was not placed on the agenda in the 1970s and sometimes arrived there only very reluctantly in the 1980s, because of patron-client politics.

There are at least three interesting questions for governance here. First, how significant are the adverse economic management implications of patronage and clientelism *compared*, for example, with ideology or policy misjudgments, in the face of an increasingly difficult external economic environment? It is not clear from recently available systematic data on policy variables such as real interest rates, budget deficits, exchange rates, how far these relate to the greater extent of patronage and clientelism that is thought to prevail in certain African countries, especially Nigeria, Ghana, Kenya, Zimbabwe compared to (say) Côte d'Ivoire, Tanzania, Malawi and Botswana. There are few estimates also of the effects of price distortions on the African economies.[10] Second, will clientelism persist, be brought under control or be undermined by changed economic conditions and market-oriented policy changes which appear to limit or reduce political intervention? Third, will any move towards political liberalisation in single-party states or greater political competition actually *encourage* clientelism and weaken economic management as it was seen to have done, for example, in Nigeria? (See also Chapter 9). It may be impossible to answer the first question though comparison of the incidence of patronage in non-African countries may throw some light on it. Chapter 9 includes some speculation on the second and third questions.

Bureaucracy and technical policy analysis

It is now fairly well established that the weaknesses of the bureaucracy have been a major factor in economic decline (see Chapter 2).[11] Our concern here is with the top level of the public administration involved in the formulation of policy rather than with its more detailed and decentralised administration. However, the former inevitably is affected by the more general malaise. Two aspects in particular are highlighted here although there are few studies of the

---

10. One estimate of the cost of rent-seeking activities to Kenya was 24% of GDP in 1982 (World Bank, 1987).

11. A recent survey of civil service weaknesses and approaches to reform in sub-Saharan Africa is Glentworth and Sparkhall, 1989. See especially Glentworth (Paper 3) and Wood (Paper 7).

'inner sanctum' of public policy-making. These are (a) the relationship with the political leadership and the degree of autonomy of the senior bureaucracy and (b) the bureaucracy as a (state) interest group influencing policy-making. There are country variations but some general perceptions emerge. Most assessments and observers assert the lack of a two-way dialogue between politicians and civil servants and the lack of independence or autonomy of African bureaucracies.

Hyden (1983), observing Tanzania in the 1970s, brings out the following features of policy-making. The civil service were not consulted on the big policy decisions but, once these had been made by party, minister or regional commissioner, they had to interpret them and devise feasible solutions. Political decisions were regarded as beyond criticism. Bureaucrats in Tanzania were aware that commitment to the policies being pursued by their political leaders was more important than offering a rational critique of these policies based on some kind of cost/benefit analysis. The non-tenured higher civil service have had to accept the blame for the failure of policy. The political leadership has therefore dominated the policy process and the civil service have not operated with autonomy, initiative or protection as in the western European model. Policy-making had over-ambitious plans and expectations which exceeded feasible delivery, and decisions were made before obtaining full and detailed knowledge of the likely consequences and without the use of past experience as a guide to the future. Where feedback of information is poor or limited, mistakes have to be of large proportion to stimulate corrective action. There are no accounts of the policy-making processes in Tanzania in the 1980s and whether it is different.

On Zambia, Wood has stated (Glentworth and Sparkhall, 1989:6):

> Economic policies have been developed by the Party without real involvement of civil servants. The rapid turnover of senior staff (which in turn affects the quality of policy analysis) is the result of decisions taken by political leaders. Numerous instances can be cited of political decision-making which has failed to take into account planning studies and which have ignored economic and administrative realities.

In Kenya an interesting difference from Tanzania in the role of patronage emerges. In Tanzania, local patrons have lost much of their influence over the administration since 1972 and this has given less protection to the masses in the rural areas from centrally decided policies that affect them adversely. In Kenya, bureaucrats, by being officially or unofficially allied with tribal and other similar associations, are key sponsors of policies benefiting members and are called upon to assist in extracting public resources for the benefits of these associations. Hence the Kenyan bureaucracy is divided, fragmented, and lacks independence and impartiality in servicing society. The president, in trying to limit these ethnic activities, reduces participation and concentrates more policy-making power in his own hands (Hyden, 1983; Barkan, 1984).

In Malawi, according to Kydd (1988:39), President Banda has had an 'attitude between scepticism and outright hostility to senior and middle management officials ... a willingness to delegate much detailed oversight of the economy to technocrats and ... to focus on key political variables such as prices and major infrastructure'. Lack of independent technical analysis of policy options and information on possible effects is stressed by Gulhati (1990:115): 'the small circle of policy makers tends to make decisions on the basis of intuition, ideology or a process of give and take'.

The lack of demand in African government for policy-relevant studies is strongly highlighted by Paul, Steedman and Sutton (1989:105):

> The attitudes of those in power within increasingly authoritarian political systems are the root cause of the lack of demand for rational data collection, analysis, financial management and planning - let alone independent policy advice from outside government. The elite in charge tends to be intolerant of scientific production in general and of policy analysis in particular .... There are no mediating forces such as opposition parties, unions or informed groups of intellectual or opinion makers who discuss and debate policy options.

The institutional environment in government service discourages the provision of policy analysis and the collection of better information, though some governments do employ individual analysts and advisers (e.g. Côte d'Ivoire, Tanzania, Ghana, Nigeria and Senegal).

Lamb (1987:18) has made the following assessment of an unnamed African country:

> A consistent and timely response to the deepening crisis was impeded by the fragmentation of information and decision-making. All major decisions ... are visibly concentrated in the person of the Head of State but many other decisions are taken in a dispersed haphazard way throughout the administration ... what planning has taken place has largely been in a formal bureaucratic sense and rarely linked to what has actually to be done to make what is planned materialise ... economic priority is granted to short term political considerations often in an disconcertingly erratic manner.

There seems to be little bureaucratic consultation of economic interest groups on policy and design, especially small producers. However, there are a few important exceptions to these generalisations.

Botswana has a rare record of effective economic management (Holm, 1988; Gulhati 1990; Harvey and Lewis, 1990). It is perhaps a special case where there has been easy two-way dialogue between political leaders and the bureaucracy and willingness on the part of the political leadership to learn from economic policy analysis and comparison with the experience of other economies. It has also relied heavily on expatriate advisers and administrators. Côte d'Ivoire has also had a good relationship between politicians and bureaucrats and an effective bureaucracy within a system of authoritarian patrimonial rule. Crook (1988) takes the view that patronage can co-exist with bureaucratic effectiveness because patrimony in Côte d'Ivoire has not been allowed to override the discipline, loyalty and role performance of the civil service. It has also gone together with 'technocratic' values determining economic policy. He attributes this to continuity between pre- and post-independence administration, a policy of gradual Ivorianisation and the 'bureaucratic' origins and composition of the political elite.

Reviewing the *process* of policy choice, Grindle and Thomas (1989) conclude, on the basis of a set of specific policy case studies (which include some from Africa), that this seems to be made on a wider range of criteria than earlier writing suggested. Technical analysis was used but was not always well understood by the political leadership. The careers and status of civil servants and departments played a significant role in institutional policy change.

In some African governments there has been a shift towards the use of more technical analysis of policy options. This has been closely linked to economic crisis and adjustment programmes in the 1980s and the influence of international financial institutions (which is considered in the next section), but it also reflects a new generation of African expertise which has been trained internationally (see Hodd, 1987).

According to Callaghy (1990) the more serious the 'crisis' is perceived to be, the more do technocratic staff influence decision-making, but these skills are quite limited in Africa. His study of Nigeria, Ghana and Zambia argues that, during the debt crisis in the late 1970s and early 1980s, small technocratic groups emerged into more prominence and influence but the degree of influence depended on the domestic political context. Technocrats had argued for 'corrective' policies during *non*-crisis periods, but had had little impact on real decisions, and only when crisis and stagnation made the rulers feel the need for corrective economic measures were they given greater prominence.

The work of both Callaghy and Grindle and Thomas suggests that the likely impact of policy choice/change on domestic political stability and support became a more important criterion in periods of crisis. Vital considerations were the range of impact, the costs and benefits, the time to implement, and the societal groups affected by the policy changes. This made certain measures like devaluation more sensitive and difficult than, say, institutional reform. However, the bureaucracy usually did not have much information on the interests of particular interest groups.

The rapid growth of state employment has provided career opportunities for members of diverse ethnic, regional and religious groups. While helping political integration, it is seen as contributing to intense pressures on national leaders to allocate public funds to ethnic groups and geographical regions roughly in proportion to their population. Bureaucratic salary structures (high in relation to GDP *per capita* at the top of the civil service), status and power, have transformed them accordingly into a powerful interest group in their own right. A number of observers see the bureaucracy as having a vested interest in, for example, over-valuation of the currency to permit them to enjoy lower import prices for their highly import-intensive patterns of consumption. They have also been opposed to any proposed reforms to reduce the size of the civil service (see Abernethy, 1988; Bates, 1981; 1988; Glentworth and Sparkhall, 1989). Grindle and Thomas (1989) stress the power of bureaucratic politics within government with regard to the selection of policy and institutional change. Decisions were made in terms of the power, links and influence of bureaucratic departments and their clienteles (e.g. informal tribal affiliations which often conflicted with formal lines of responsibility). Parastatal officials and managers often constitute a powerful and privileged class able to manipulate government policy in their own interests, not through conventional participation but instead by incorporation of these interests into the government itself.

The role of parties and parliaments

Tordoff (1984) in his general review of African political parties takes the view that their role has often been limited to that of ratifying decisions taken elsewhere. This he attributes to (a) the trend towards single-party rule, with competitive parties surviving only in The

Gambia, Botswana and Mauritius; (b) increased personalisation of power; (c) the subordination of the party to the state; (d) the weakness of interest groups which 'tend to lack resources to command leverage'; and (e) the demoralisation of the party, the indifferent quality of party personnel and the increasingly technical nature of economic activity.

The literature on African *single-party* systems brings out the weak organisational base of parties at the grass-roots level. The party system has not proved a strong instrument of mobilisation and social transformation (Callaghy, 1986). Also, the contradictions of society are 'internalised' within the state apparatus and to allow challenges from separate political voices then risks the disintegration of the state. Perhaps most important of all, parties are seen as mechanisms of control, not consultation.

Criticism of existing policy and the circulation of new or alternative policy ideas do not seem to have developed significantly within single parties so far, even in that limited number of countries which are recognised as having *intra-party* competition - viz. Kenya, Côte d'Ivoire, Zambia and Mozambique (Sandbrook, 1985). Ambitions beyond those of their clans on the part of political leaders are seen as a threat to the party supremo; the 'arena of participation has been shrunk to the walls of the single party' and there has been a limit on how much participation a party can tolerate. In this situation it has been difficult for alternative policies and widened policy agendas to be aired openly and politically (Hyden, 1983).

Even in two countries - Tanzania and Kenya - where electoral systems have survived under single parties, the roles of elected representatives both collectively and individually emerge as weak in relation to national policy-making, and the electoral process does not provide voters with a choice of policy alternatives or governing elites (Hopkin, 1979; Barkan, 1984).

In Kenya, political participation is by means of an electoral process that selects representatives to link the periphery with the centre in the allocation of state resources. This political participation is primarily in order to gain access to resources and not to change the leadership, the national policies or development objectives. The power of the party as a policy-making institution has been cumulatively reduced and passed to an oligarchy consisting of the president, cabinet ministers and state officials. The legislative assembly is not an arena for the deliberation and making of policy. Individual MPs have found that attention paid to national policy issues and actions rather than local lobbying for resources is most likely to lose them their seats. Meanwhile, the detention without trial of MPs who criticise proposed government policy or actions has inhibited parliamentary willingness to question policy made by the executive.

In Tanzania, in the 1960s the single-party TANU had the power to lay down the broad lines of policy. Conflicts were resolved in private under the party umbrella and bargaining took place on policy issues behind closed doors. Later the President came to dominate over the Chairman within the NEC, but van Donge and Liviga (1986) see the political culture of consensus as inhibiting cabinet ministers of long standing from taking an independent stand on policy issues within the cabinet or in public.

Their more recent study (van Donge and Liviga, 1989) of the Tanzanian parliament and parliamentary elections in the 1980s stresses these as one of the few platforms where the government is publicly criticised and elections are genuinely competitive. MPs have been openly very critical of the limits on parliamentary power to defeat the executive. On the other hand, it confirms that parliament is marginal in the policy-making process and the focus of the elections is on personalities and not policies or programmes. Indeed, the announcement and implementation of quite radical economic policy changes - decontrol of markets and prices and greater scope for private accumulation, 1980-5 - by-passed parliament and received little public debate. Nor did these ideological changes feature in the party, the constituency or the elections. These changes appear to have been popular, but it is less clear, as van Donge and Liviga argue, that they were made by the government in response to popular demand.

Le Vine (1979) concluded that, in Francophone Africa, the legislatures had simply become another instrument of the ruling elites which was dispensable if not useful to them. The national assembly served as a patronage function to co-opt would-be counter-elites and ensure loyalty to the regime. Its contribution to development policy was ineffective and circumscribed by the wishes of the political leadership.

An important question, then, is whether in modern African 'one-party' or 'no-party' states, most of which began their existence with elected assemblies, it is possible to revive or enhance the role of the legislature and of individual elected MPs in order to ensure greater consultation, exposure, and scrutiny of public policy and its implementation. Or is it really essential for multi-party systems to re-emerge?

What has been the experience of *multi-party systems* or episodes in Africa for economic management? Both Botswana and Mauritius have had multi-party political systems and dynamic economies over quite long periods. Yet there have been others in which democratic openings were accompanied by an acceleration of economic decline rather than any revival and growth - Ghana, 1979-81, Nigeria, 1979-83, and Sudan, 1985-89. Botswana and Ghana perhaps illustrate the extremes.

Botswana has had multi-party constitutional rule for more than two decades. It scores well not just on democratic politics but also on sound and prudent economic policies and a consistently high economic growth performance. It has had one of the highest long-run growth rates in Africa, one of the best records of public sector management, prudent macroeconomic management, moderate exchange rates, and moderate state intervention. How are these qualities seen to be related by scholars? Recent studies have been made by Holm (1988) and Harvey and Lewis (1990).

Botswana has had regular elections and opposition parties since 1965, though the opposition have rarely gained more than a small minority of seats. There are limits on who may run for parliament and on the degree of criticism of government, and the opposition parties lack finance. Also there is minimal organised interest-group activity. According to Holm (1988) in all the elections the parties have shown little interest in raising and debating policy issues. Issues have played a declining role over time and the opposition parties have not focused on serious alternative policy agendas. The competition has been between ethnic leaders for a fair distribution of the state's resources, though the ruling party has been careful to distribute the benefits of government programmes equitably in order to diffuse tribal criticism. Patronage and corruption have been well controlled by a rigorous system of accounting controls and independent audit under the supervision of the National Assembly, but its role has been a passive one in policy-making. On this evaluation, political competition and democratic procedures in Botswana are not seen as a key explanation of the country's relatively good economic policy and performance; rather, the latter gives legitimacy to a ruling political class and a highly trained, autonomous bureaucracy (Diamond, 1988).

Not all observers see it this way. Most recognise the importance in Botswana's case of a political culture or tradition of 'consensus' which marks it out among many African societies (Gulhati, 1990). Under this tradition, policy change has proceeded cautiously, incrementally and by extensive consultation especially with those affected on major policy initiatives, thus giving the country stability and continuity. An important feature of policy formulation was the attention paid to the experience of other countries. Whether the general prudence and economic rationality of the policies directly relate to consensus and consultation or whether they stem from some other element in the culture does not emerge clearly from the literature. However, in a recent major study, Harvey and Lewis (1990) bring out the fact that the electoral process in a predominantly rural population made the ruling regime responsive to rural interests while being made aware by the urban constituencies of too much policy imbalance, and thus induced efforts to ensure a reasonable distribution of income and public services. On this reading Botswana sets a model for 'good' governance and economic management. But it is perhaps a special case, being small, with good mineral endowment, and geographically very close to the South African economy.

Ghana has had a mixture of military and civil, authoritarian and democratic regimes since independence and is perhaps an interesting controlled experiment for the way economic policy and performance fare under different types of political regime and single and multi-party systems. This experience has been recently reviewed by Chazan (1988a). Her evaluation brings out the fact that the democratic regimes, though different in circumstances of power, party structure, constitutional safeguards, and specific ideology, all evinced a marked inability to manage the economy and to sustain levels of mobilisation and participation over time. Democratically elected leaders adopted and defended a more capitalist and gradualist approach to development than authoritarian regimes. Both have had inadequate mechanisms for policy formation or control over policy-makers and both types of regime were overthrown under the strains of popular discontent and economic mismanagement.

Democratic regimes have, in varying measure, protected civil and political rights and freedom of association, while authoritarian rule was more explicitly repressive and coercive. At the same time the democratic governments have generally been weaker and less forceful in the pursuit of their goals and have supported greater inequalities. Neither type of regime has been able to strike deep roots. Both have been unable to withstand partisan pressures from below. Decision-makers have been exposed to specific sectional interests from those selective solidarity groups in the ruling coalitions.

Chazan sees the democratic ethos as locally strong in Ghana - with an ingrained local culture of consultation, participation and supervision of authority. The failure to sustain an effective and representative government is attributed to a centralised state with bureaucratic structures and personalised decision-taking without consultation and compromise. During the periods of democratic rule, party structures which rest on patronage networks deliberately excluded major groups from representation in the ruling coalition, hence reducing legitimacy and longevity. Because 'too much is at stake' for those in power (in terms of control over resources), national politics came to 'matter too much' and tolerance for the opposition was too low.

These features - intolerance of criticism, unwillingness to consult or seek consensus, and exclusivity - by all types of regimes, whether elected or not, seem to have been associated with poor economic policy-making in the 1970s. Therein lies the interesting contrast with Botswana.

Before summarising the essential features of the policy-making process in Africa in the 1970s we turn, in the next chapter, from the state-centred perspective to interpretations of the influence of interest groups - domestic and external - on policy-making.

5
Interest Groups, External Actors and Policy Change in the 1980s

In this chapter we take a 'society-centred' perspective on interest groups in Africa and on interpretations of their role in policy formation in the 1970s in particular. We then turn to the *changes* in policy orientation of a number of countries in the mid-1980s and assess how far these are explained by domestic forces as compared with the role of external financial agencies.

Interest groups in Africa: general perceptions

Many African countries have a long tradition of independent associational activity which has provided a counterpart to the authoritarian trends prevalent in the post-colonial period. A distinction is sometimes made in the literature between modern interest groups organised around economic issues, and traditional communal organisations based on kinship, region and ethnicity, although some of these modern associational structures derive their impetus from traditional institutions for protecting collective interests and resolving disputes (Rothchild and Foley, 1988).

Numerous sectoral and class-based organisations which cut across ethno-regional boundaries (especially labour unions, peasant movements and professional associations) were formed in the colonial period, partly in response to the process of urbanisation and commercialisation, and some of them became actively involved in the struggle against colonial rule (Bratton, 1989). After independence, many of these organisations were absorbed into state and party structures or were suppressed. Since all societal cleavages were treated as illegitimate by authoritarian regimes, the activities of independent ethnic associations were channelled into single-party activity in the interest of preserving political order and achieving national unity (Callaghy, 1986; Lonsdale, 1981). As noted by Hodder-Williams (1984:104):

> They were not only organisations through which people expressed their political aspirations but they provided a ready-made base for a political

machine, offering a range of benefits to their members and votes for the leaders.

In this way, ethno-regional interest groups did achieve a measure of political representation but mainly through informal arrangements such as balanced representation and co-optation in cabinet positions. Their supporters were able to secure benefits through a process of clientelism described earlier (see Chapters 2 and 4). These mechanisms also provided representation to class and functional interests (Joseph, 1983), although Rothchild and Foley (1988) argue that modern interest groups tend to be less influential politically than the communal ones or to be excluded altogether. According to Callaghy (1986), the exclusive single-party apparatus was intended to limit political participation, although in some countries voluntary organisations were able to retain a degree of independence and provided a space for organisational activity outside the domain of the state.

An independent and vibrant press also widens the scope for the expression of opinions and ideas outside the realm of the state. Despite attempts by the state to muzzle dissent by closing down publications, arresting journalists and imposing strict censorship, the press continued to play a vigorous role in exposing the seamy side of politics in a few countries such as Nigeria, despite the closure of formal channels for organised political opposition.

There is considerable variation in the degree of institutionalisation and richness of civil society in different countries, reflecting both historical and cultural factors and the coercive power of the state. In Ghana, for example, interest groups comprising intellectuals, business and professional associations, students, trade unions and religious organisations have had an active involvement in challenging state domination and tyranny (Chazan, 1988a). By contrast, in autocratic states such as Malawi, the political space for independent interest group activity is highly circumscribed. Societal discontent is expressed through forms of disengagement from state structures (migration, smuggling, informal markets, etc.) or non-compliance (refusal to market certain crops, declining productivity) (Azarya, 1988). As stated by Bayart (1986:119), 'societies chip away at the state "from below" rather than through organised challenge', which explains the relatively low level of organised political resistance to state dominance in Africa, at least until recently.

Reviews of the influence of civil society on state action and policy include the work of political scientists like Bates (1981, 1988), Chabal (1986), Chazan and Rothchild (1988), and political economists like

Mosley *et al.* (1991). Much case-study research with a pluralist perspective has been done on advanced democratic societies. More limited research has been carried out in Africa, partly, but not entirely, because political influence and the lobbying process is more informal and less visible than in developed countries such as the USA or UK (Chabal, 1986; Grindle and Thomas, 1989). Nevertheless some quite strong perceptions emerge about both (a) general state/civil society relations and (b) the relative importance of specific interest groups. We distinguish interest groups and their influence on state policy as separable from, but overlapping with, patron-client relationships. The latter tend to be more personal and disaggregated and to be seen as less important in their influence on policy design than on administration, the implementation of policy and the use of state revenues (see, e.g., Sandbrook, 1986; Grindle and Thomas, 1989).

The following points emerge from the literature: a pattern of policy driven by societal interests, with the state as a more or less neutral arena in which competitive lobbies fight for control of policy resources as in Western polyarchies, is very little in evidence in Africa.

> No one understands interest group representation in any African country particularly well since it needs an accurate understanding of the political motivations of specific interest groups and the process of lobbying which for elite organisations is not very public, rather informal and can involve rather delicate ethnic issues (Dunn, 1986:165).

> The main focus of ethno-regional interest groupings tends to be distribution of services such as health care, education, transport and communication, investment, targeted development funds and civil service recruitment. The economic/class interest groups are more likely to focus on tax policy, credit lines, subsidies, and protection (Rothchild and Foley, 1988).

Organised interest groups and their input into the political system are still relatively weak, especially the broad-based ones like trade unions, while commercial interests tend to find more direct means of access to relevant persons in the state apparatus (Berg-Schlosser, 1984). People have more capacity to influence policy implementation than policy formation (i.e. via evasion, bending rules, bribes to the bureaucracy, etc.). Interest groups are seen as lacking resources to command leverage and interact with government (Tordoff, 1984). For example, neither Malawi nor Madagascar has highly organised and formal sets of interest groups which lobby the government for particular economic policies. According to Pryor (1990), the informal influence of families and personalities as well as trading and agricultural estate interests and those of the military are more pronounced in Madagascar, but these groups seldom develop a single unified position on public policy.

There are few agreed rules in the game of political competition - written or unwritten. Since minority ethnic or communal interests cannot expect any change from the majority there is a tendency for permanent minorities to be created. This can generate secessionist or violent action rather than pressures for the adjustment of policies.

Despite much scholarly attention to 'urban bias' in African policy-making (see below), Mosley *et al.* (1991) in their study of policy reform in the 1980s (which included Kenya, Ghana, Malawi as well as some non-African countries) found little evidence of urban coalitions, either between industrialists or between industrialists and workers; nor was the rural sector weak or disenfranchised. Worker (mainly urban) resistance to policy change has been small in most cases. Large farmers, on the other hand, were politically influential in countries like Kenya.

Political participation and pressure in the form of the urban riot has been studied in West Africa by Wiseman (1986) for the 1977-85 period. Riots in towns and cities have been far more common, larger-scale and more effective than in rural areas. Students were the most common participants. The most general cause was the unpopularity of corrupt, incompetent and authoritarian regimes. The violence arose mainly from the actions of the state elite. This confirms the more general experience that political violence, via repression, is more likely where there is less political (electoral) accountability (Nelson 1987).

Wiseman's evidence suggests that riots were rarely effective in bringing about change in government policy, though there were two interesting cases - relating to food pricing and marketing policy - where change was induced. Regimes have been changed primarily via coup d'états in West African states but violent urban protests contributed to the ensuing overthrow of regimes in at least four cases. Wiseman concludes that the threat to regime survival from urban riots was rather limited. However, some observers think this picture may be changing as popular pressures and protests in favour of greater democracy and human rights have increased since the late 1980s.

Specific interest groups

Indigenous business class

Some scholars see the greatest weakness of civil society in counter-vailing or disciplining the power of the state as lying in the absence of an independent and robust bourgeoisie (see Hyden, 1983; Sandbrook, 1985). Most observers view the indigenous business class in Africa as weak, embryonic and lacking in independence because it has usually grown up under the protection and privileged support of the state elite. However, some scholars distinguish between business groups which lack autonomy like those in Côte d'Ivoire, Zaire and Sierra Leone, and those which have some independence as in Kenya, Senegal, Nigeria and Cameroon (Bayart, 1986).

As organised interest groups, business has sought less to shape broad policy than to seek exceptions, modifications, delays or other concessions in the *application* of policies to their specific firms (Sandbrook, 1985). When gradual import liberalisation is introduced business interests tend to pick away at its implementation through myriad administrative and political channels (Nelson, 1990). In sub-Saharan Africa, where much business is controlled by ethnic and alien minorities, this approach may be seen also as politically more sensitive than collective efforts to block or alter general policies.

A second aspect is that the interests of businesses are *heterogenous* and often conflicting, especially as between exporters and companies processing or manufacturing for the home market. They do not seem always to know where their own real long-term interests lie (Skalnes, 1989; Callaghy, 1990). Outside South Africa, industrialists rarely constitute a unified pressure group on trade policy except in so far as they all want to operate at lower cost. On the output side there is usually no coherent position on liberalisation within the Chamber of Industries or its equivalent and there is frequently special pleading by makers of particular products (see Mosley *et al.*, 1991).

Many industrialists, who have benefitted from protection by the state, have not favoured privatisation or deregulation. Nelson (1990) reports little support among African business for devaluation, trade liberalisation or, less surprisingly, for higher interest rates. However, in Nigeria most indigenous businessmen and the transnationals favoured IMF stabilisation programmes by 1985, but with the large-scale farmers lobbying behind the scenes. However, only the National Association of Manufacturers declared itself publicly in favour of IMF stabilisation while protesting against import liberalisation. In Nigeria (1985) and also Zambia (1983 and 1986), it was the exporters and those who needed foreign exchange who supported the negotiation of an IMF stabilisation package (Martin, 1991).

Industrial working class and trade unions

Industrial workers in Africa have not been successful in securing effective political representation or in influencing the policy agenda. The reasons for this include (a) the fact that the small industrial proletariat and its rural ties in most countries have weakened radical consciousness; (b) urban labour markets are slack; (c) governments have been repressive of dissident labour organisations or have co-opted trade union leaders; and (d) trade unions and industrial workers are generally not organised as a whole and have rarely delayed or modified adjustment policies (Mosley *et al.*, 1991).

National labour movements have exerted considerable, if fleeting, pressure in particular countries (Guinea, Ghana, Nigeria, Zambia). But enduring representation of their interests was achieved only in certain localised industrial unions such as the Zambian and Ghanaian miners (Dunn, 1986; Nelson, 1990). Government economic policy (especially on pricing and wages) has been delayed or drastically modified when there was a broader coalition of trade unions and urban middle and business classes, as in Zambia in 1986.

Medium peasants/larger farmers

All scholars agree on the essential political weakness of peasants or small farmers in Africa. Hyden (1983) takes the view that the peasant producers do not need the state since they have limited dependence on markets and limited technology, and so can and do easily 'exit' from the formal economy. For him this low level of interdependence on the part of a basically pre-capitalist class discourages the bargaining approach to politics which is a pre-condition of democracy.

Bates (1981) takes the same view, that peasants form a weak interest group, and seek to 'exit' from official marketing and government policies (via subsistence agriculture, crop switches, smuggling, migration) rather than voicing their concerns collectively. He places much weight on the large number of them in scattered locations and the high costs for them of lobbying, organisation, negotiation and communication. Herbst (1990) takes the view that the opportunities for poor African agriculturalists to 'exit' by migration are becoming increasingly limited, and thinks that there will be political consequences if they exercise their 'voice' instead.

However, both Bates and Mosley *et al.* (1991) recognise that the larger farmers (though fewer in numbers) constitute a powerful lobby. In several African countries they are strongly organised and often form a politically influential interest group. A distinction is made between communal farmers predominantly selling in the home market (food and raw materials) and those who predominantly export, although the latter have not necessarily dominated over other interests. (The cocoa farmers in Ghana were thought to have 'lost out' to urban consumer and other interests in the past (Rimmer, 1986).)

Other interest and pressure groups

The establishment of one-party systems in Africa has usually suppressed the independence of the press to comment on and criticise government policy. Examples are Malawi and Zaire. However, before the recent return to multi-party democracy, Zambia offered evidence that the press (and the church) were able to play an effective if partial role as open critics of government action and occasionally as modifiers of state policy (Lungu, 1986). Lungu explained the acceptance of open and public criticism in Zambia as due to the particular personality of President Kaunda, the long history of public debate and criticism (predating independence) and the particular etiquette or style of criticism which has been accepted by both rulers and critics. Provided this etiquette was observed, critics were free to attack the entire leadership collectively or to single out individual leaders and the policies of particular departments as long as the head of state was not directly attacked. Despite this there does not seem to have been much evidence of the general effectiveness of open criticism in the evolution of Zambian economic policy though the church and the unions undoubtedly modified some specific policy stances of the Kaunda government (e.g. population policy and wage and price policy).

Interest-group interpretations of policy

The literature exploring the impact of these interest groups on policy formation in Africa is rather limited and suffers from a number of weaknesses. First, it provides very uneven coverage. There is quite a considerable amount of exploration of the political determinants of agricultural policies (e.g. Bates, 1981; Rondinelli, 1986). Trade policy has also been examined from a more pluralist perspective by Mosley *et al.* (1991) in a study of trade regime reform that covers some African case studies. Nevertheless there is singularly little written on the politics of several other aspects of African policy, e.g., the pattern of taxation, public expenditure allocation or the politics of financial policies.

Second, the work done by Bates (1981, 1988) gives important insights into the configuration of African policy established during the 1960s and 1970s. The Bates thesis on African agricultural policy is now well-known. In a detailed and subtle analysis he sees this as a response to the interests of a mainly urban-based coalition of industrial business (owners and workers) and senior civil servants, whose key and common interest is seen as low domestic prices for food and agricultural raw materials since this lowers their wage and import costs as well as serving urban consumer interests. The policy complex which delivers such as outcome is seen as monopsonistic state marketing; the setting of low food procurement prices or low prices to the urban consumer via subsidies; and overvalued exchange rates to reduce the costs of imported food, raw materials, and consumer goods while protecting industrial output for the domestic market by means of quotas and tariffs. The larger farmers who are seen as part of this coalition and who might otherwise lose by lower food prices are also postulated as being 'bought-off' by subsidised inputs (e.g. for credit and fertiliser). Public services are used to gain political support in the countryside through the allocation of projects such as roads, schools, water supplies, to certain areas, whether they are economically justified or not.

What are the politics of this policy syndrome? Bates (1981) sees the governing elite as maintaining power by seeking a coalition of groups who will support them in return for benefits or 'economic rents', and privileges. It is not therefore a *passive* response to interest-group pressures as in pluralist political theory. It is clientelism; the state elite seek support from the most powerful organised interest groups in society, such as large estate farmers as well as large businesses, which are able to exert pressure on government more effectively than (say) the small farmers dispersed throughout the countryside. Appeasement of these interests along the above lines is seen as the alternative to repression or co-optation, especially of trade union leaders or officials, although both approaches have often gone together.

This agricultural policy pattern fitted quite a number of African countries in the 1970s (e.g. Ghana and Nigeria), although it has been contested whether it fitted Côte d'Ivoire (Hecht, 1983) or Zimbabwe (Herbst, 1989) or, for that matter, Malawi and Kenya. Where it prevailed, it clearly had an adverse effect on agricultural output and small farmers often 'evaded' the policies by switching crops, moving into subsistence, smuggling or migrating - a major factor in economic decline in Africa.

Bates' interpretation therefore provides a powerful insight into how 'coalition rational' policy design can work strongly against 'economically rational' policies and the collective interest. However, a number of questions must be raised about this interpretation of African experience and its implications.[12]

There is some inconsistency in an interpretation that places such weight on societal interests and pressures when so many observers have stressed the weakness and limited independence of civil society organisations in Africa. For example, if there was a weak indigenous business class in the 1960s, how were pressures for industrial protection organised? Mosley *et al.* (1991) apparently found little evidence of urban coalitions between industrialists and labour or among industrialists in their study of policy reform.

There is also some lack of *dynamics* in this interpretation of politics. It does not really explain why policy *change* takes place as opposed to explaining the policy pattern of *some* African countries at a certain period of history (primarily in the 1970s). There is insufficient attention to 'feedback' which may correct inappropriate policy not via organised political pressure but via the options of 'exit' or 'evasion', on the part of those affected by the policy. This is recognised but not given adequate weight.[13] Although it may have been a slow process, policies did change significantly in the mid-1980s in several African countries (see World Bank, 1990 and below).

---

12. For a recent summary and critique of Bates see Skalnes (1989). His method of approach is based on *inference* rather than *empirical* work to establish precisely how these coalitions formed, how these interest groups individually formulated their objectives, organised themselves and how they brought their influence to bear. There is 'anecdotal' evidence. Perhaps patronage and clientelism are difficult to observe directly and to document. However, there is not enough systematic testing of policy configuration (across countries) and policy change within them over time. Indeed, there seem to be few direct studies of specific interest group organisation and tactics in African conditions; the process does seem to be fairly 'invisible' (see Dunn, 1986; Grindle, 1989).

13. A good example would be the use by the government of food marketing boards in Tanzania in the 1970s to set low producer prices (perhaps for the reasons that Bates suggests). However, in practice the policy proved to be self-defeating since it was met by a reduced supply response, disappointed urban consumers, and the development of parallel markets at high prices. The government reversed its low-price policy in the early 1980s. (See Arhin, Hesp and van der Lann (1985) for the limits to government policy via marketing boards).

Policy change in the 1980s: domestic and external forces

By the mid-1980s, significant policy change was taking place in some African countries despite the rather static, pessimistic view taken by a wide range of political observers and scholars. Some of these, however, believe it is too soon to speak of sustainable economic reform or reversal of the policy patterns we have reviewed earlier.

The extent to which the economic policy agenda has changed, and institutional, macroeconomic and microeconomic policies have changed permanently, is still debated. Nevertheless, there was more radical, general and specific, policy change in late 1980s than in the 1970s and various World Bank reports document this for Africa (see especially World Bank, 1989a, 1989b, 1990b). By 1987, 28 African countries had major economic reform and adjustment planned or under way.

The main changes in the 1980s have been: (a) a major realignment of real effective exchange rates; (b) liberalisation of external trade; (c) deregulation of domestic and external trade by relaxing state monopsony and monopoly marketing; (d) a rise in real producer prices and reduced 'taxation' of agricultural export crops and food crops; (e) stabilisation of the size of the public enterprise sector which in some countries was reduced; (f) modest reforms of financial policy. There has as yet, however, been no systematic improvement in fiscal balances; revenue has stagnated, and public expenditure has not been compressed.

There have been significant country variations. Some (e.g. Sudan) have not embarked on reforms. The World Bank (1989a, 1989b, 1990b) has made the following evaluation. Some countries have produced still-born or stalled economic reform programmes (e.g. Somalia, Zaire and Zambia). Others embarked on reforms late in the 1980s (e.g. Tanzania, Nigeria and Mozambique). The strongest, earliest and so far most consistent reforms have been in Ghana, Madagascar, Togo, Malawi and Kenya, while continuing good economic management has been a feature of Botswana, Mauritius and Côte d'Ivoire.

How have these changes in policy - often considerable reversals of past patterns and even ideology - been explained politically?

The range of explanations fall broadly into two classifications: those which see the main influence as the *external* agencies - primarily the IMF and the World Bank and the bilateral aid agencies - and those which look at the *domestic* balance of political and social forces at work.[14]

The international financial agencies

For some time there have been voices which see African economic policy as effectively controlled from Washington. More recently Joseph (1989:116) has stated:

> The African post-colonial state which has sought to determine the utilisation of its people's economic resources, has in many instances become a 'rubber stamp' for decisions made by others, usually non-African in nationality .... The decision-making powers of aid agencies in Africa have expanded as a result of the default of those who man the 'political kingdoms'.... There is taking place an implicit loss of sovereignty desirable in some instances, in view of the misuse of it by those in power.

Some would see the reversal of past ideology or policy patterns in Africa and the new greater emphasis on monetary and fiscal stabilisation and market-oriented reform programmes as *prima facie* evidence of external influence, especially on the part of the World Bank/IMF. Few are likely to disagree with Abernethy (1989) that there has been a steady loss of effective African control over decision-making in a wide range of policy areas in the 1980s, or probably with the Carter Center (1989) that the IFIs have come to wield unprecedented influence over African economic policies and institutions in the 1980s.[15]

First, the bilateral donors became more co-ordinated, forming a consensus around programme aid linked to macroeconomic conditions which did not exist in the 1960s and 1970s when donors competed to provide project funds. What is more, the leading IFIs have been powerful lobbyists for funds from bilateral donors (e.g. at consultative group meetings) and commercial creditors and because they are often successful they carry even greater weight on policy change with the

---

14. There is now a considerable body of case-study research and interpretation of adjustment policies in the 1980s which covers some African countries. These include Grindle and Thomas, 1989; Callaghy, 1986, 1990; Nelson, 1990; Herbst, 1989; Skalnes, 1989; Martin, 1989; Fearon, 1988; Shams, 1989; Harvey, 1990; Mosley *et al.*, 1991; Gulhati, 1990; Killick, 1990.

15. The *trend* towards increased IFI and donor influence stems from a number of developments which are set out in recent working papers published by the Carter Center (1989).

African recipient governments whose bargaining power has weakened over time.

Second, several African regimes, which have wished to cling to power in the face of internal and external financial 'crisis', have been seen as able to do so by settling for IFI conditions and access to finance.

Third, external (including IFI) economic advisers have played a key and increasing role in policy analysis as African capacity has often been lacking at a time of challenging problems. Certain domestic groups in the political leadership and in the bureaucracy have secured powerful positions with external support, while the IFI training and overseas education of certain African personnel have imported a technocratic and more market-oriented economic philosophy.

If the shift in bargaining power over time towards external influence is generally accepted, there is nevertheless the more debatable issue of whether external or domestic influence has predominated in the 1980s change in domestic economic strategies, in a number of countries. The two major studies of adjustment which tackle this question on the basis of adjustment case studies going beyond those in Africa are Nelson (1990), and Mosley *et al.* (1991). Nelson concludes (1990:330-31) that external agencies were less important than domestic political forces in determining the *timing and scope* of adjustment decisions:

> Concerted pressures from IFIs, bilateral donors and commercial banks ... play prominent roles in the tales of all our cases. But the degree to which such pressures actually induced decisions *that would not otherwise have been taken varied greatly* .... External pressures had greatest influence on the timing and scope of adjustment decisions with governments which were divided or indecisive but had sufficient authority to take action (e.g. Kaunda and Zambia in 1983) .... For Rawlings and Babangida it was impossible to imagine the same decisions in the absence of external advice and pressure.

Nelson recognises that IFI alumni played a key role in a dual political game: interpreting external pressures and trying to persuade domestic colleagues. Moreover, some senior economic officials and influential economists in the countries which were undertaking adjustment had spent some time as staff members of the IMF and the World Bank. Martin (1991:65) also concludes that most sub-Saharan African governments which approached the IMF saw the need for policy change.

On the *content* of policy, limited African analytical capacity was seen as constraining domestic ability to formulate detailed alternatives to the IFI proposals; the latter therefore had influence by default. From the standpoint of the individual government, external agencies were seen as playing a major, and often domineering, role in the implementation of orthodox stabilisation policies, *but* external pressure was not very important in explaining the variation between the implementation and abandonment of stabilisation programmes. The degree of implementation was not related to the scale of external finance or the depth or detail of the external involvement, advice and guidance. Ultimately domestic politics set the basic parameters of government efforts to carry out adjustment programmes (Nelson, 1990:342).

This view seems to be echoed by Mosley *et al.* (1991) who thought the World Bank had weak influence in countries undertaking structural adjustment. It could not 'coerce' reforms. Loan conditions were often 'soft' and no tough punishment regime existed for non-compliance. Indeed, compliance with conditions overall was seen as very problematic. The level of a country's financial dependence on the Bank appears to have exercised little influence on the degree of 'slippage' on policy conditions of policy (Kenya and Malawi, for example, with high levels of financial assistance experienced serious slippage).

Fearon (1988) takes an even bolder line in rejecting the argument that policy changes in the 1980s were 'coerced' by the external agencies. In his view, the African leaders shared with the international community common norms about sovereignty, the role of the state and the goals of government. African leaders were seeking (a) to put their legitimacy and authority on a firmer footing and (b) to bring under the purview of central government a bureaucracy lost to the parallel market, and (c) were accepting a change in ideology which represented a learning-process recognising the validity of outside criticism of domestic economic policies. Rulers aiming at policy reform are seen by Fearon as 'realists' using the finance of the IFIs and donors to prevent the total disintegration of their state and their authority, and to restore the strength and competitiveness of their own economies. Ghana, Guinea, Sierra Leone, Tanzania are seen as examples of such self-determined initiatives.

There are others, however, (e.g. Bierstecker, 1990) who consider it premature to judge the issue of major policy change. The real test is the sustainable implementation of economic policy and constitutional change but the evidence for this is as yet inconclusive since it depends on the likelihood of continuing domestic political support. We turn therefore to domestic political interpretations of adjustment policies.

Domestic politics of policy reform

There have been a whole range of political explanations of the background to economic reforms in the 1980s. These include the following: (a) perceived crisis or limits of decline; (b) learning from past mistakes and ideology reversal; (c) different types of political regimes, new regimes and consultation; (d) the character of the political leadership; and (e) the shift in the balance of power between interest groups and the degree of state 'insulation' from societal pressures. Not all these are mutually exclusive explanations; indeed several of them are often combined in single studies and interpretations. Political scientists rarely set out their formal framework for approaching explanations of this kind even though they implicitly follow one.[16]

Most interpretations give much attention to 'crisis', which was not only perceived by African rulers by the end of the 1970s, but was rooted in objective, major and persistent changes in circumstances (poor international trade prospects, terms of trade deterioration, acute debt-service burdens, domestic economic decline, fiscal imbalance and the undermining of government finance through the growth in parallel economies, etc.). Crisis situations forced certain policy issues on to the *agenda* which would probably not have been chosen in less pressing

---

16. Two recently proposed analytical frameworks are both by economists. Killick (1990) sees major economic change as the outcome of a (deteriorating) balance of political and economic costs and benefits. The point at which change takes place depends on the societal distribution of the impact of the change, the likely speed and duration of the impact, the weight attached to the affected groups, and the resources and scope for compensating the losers.

Toye (1991) has a more institutional framework. Whether there is specific policy change depends on (a) the degree to which interest groups succeed in organising themselves in favour of or against proposed reform and (b) the 'opacity' of formal state/political institutions and their informal ideological apparatus which determines the scope for exercising influence. These influences differ between countries and the balance of forces within them. Clearly these are not easily testable propositions about the strength of interests and the resistance of the state. Callaghy (1990) adopts a similar perspective in a study of reforms in Ghana, Zambia and Nigeria, where he sees the degree of autonomy of the state as dependent not only on socio-political organisation and pressure but also on the nature of the 'crisis'.

circumstances. The crisis was the challenge to make changes - structural rather than incremental - where the alternative of 'no change' was perceived to have worse consequences for those in power (Fearon, 1988). This 'trough factor' was a threat to political stability as well as to regime survival and legitimacy and to state authority. The 'desperation' thesis, however, is seen as a necessary rather than sufficient condition for major policy reversal.

The 'learning process' of regimes is given weight by a number of scholars, though few support the view that ideological reversal is genuinely taking place in countries other than those where the reforms reflect an existing ideological disposition in favour of a market economy (i.e. Nigeria, Kenya, Malawi, Mauritius). The World Bank, for example, found that among different countries there was no correlation between the intensity of policy reform under Structural Adjustment Loans and the pre-existing level of economic distortions (Mosley *et al.*, 1991:41). More work on ideological change in response to the policy reform in countries like Madagascar, Mozambique, Tanzania and Ghana would be useful. Several observers felt that there was little alternative for countries in these crisis situations (e.g. Green and Colclough, 1988; Martin, 1989), and that ideological reversal could be discounted at this stage.[17]

The influence of the type of political regime on stabilisation and structural reform is explored in a number of recent studies covering African and other developing countries. The specific thesis that authoritarian government is more effective in making unpopular radical change, has also been recently evaluated by scholars (Nelson, 1990; Callaghy, 1990; Mosley *et al.*, 1991). There seems little foundation for the view that authoritarian regimes are more likely to *embark* on radical economic reform, although some have done so (see Chapter 7).

It seems to be the strength or weakness of the regime - whatever its complexion - which appears to influence the decisiveness or delay. Weak governments/central executives which are unable to command support from divided parties, coalitions, or key support groups guarantee delay and paralysis on economic reform and in any case usually produce narrow agendas (e.g. Kaunda in 1983). Where there are strong executives with wide support or a splintered opposition, the

---

17. The Rawlings regime in Ghana abandoned Marxism in the early 1980s but continues to express a populist agenda while at the same time implementing economic policy reforms.

initiation of broad programmes of reforms are more likely but are not guaranteed.

New regimes committed to change have at least initial advantages (e.g. Rawlings in Ghana, and Conte in Guinea). New presidents facilitated change in Tanzania, but with less commitment in Sierra Leone. However, the emergence of new brooms did not always ensure that they would sweep clean (Mosley *et al.*, 1991; Lukes and Riley, 1988).

Consultation by referendum or elections in both single party and multi-party systems has tended to reduce the autonomy of the regime and to weaken support for stabilisation and economic reform efforts, as in Zambia in 1983, while Babangida's consultation and planned transition back to civilian democracy in Nigeria seems to have weakened the impetus to work at restructuring. Callaghy (1990) sees military governments as more insulated than civilian ones and brings out the point that public debate in Nigeria revealed a low general level of public understanding of the issues and that the regime's promise of a transition to democracy *before* the economic reforms weakened the required insulation of the state. Badly organised and executed local (non-party) elections became a platform for attacks on the regime and on economic reform. Only the political skill of the leadership enabled the economic reforms to be embarked on.

An acute problem in reconciling major stabilisation and structural adjustment policies with consultation and democracy, is that the policy measures are unlikely to make a favourable impact fast enough. Harvey (1990) draws attention to the speed and extent to which devaluation improves the budget, as a factor affecting the sustainability of reforms. In Mauritius, however, Shams (1989) brings out how there was consensus on the implementation of an adjustment programme in a democratic system largely because the programme did not imply a radical change in policy - merely a consistent application of strategies already agreed for some time (cf. Bowman, 1991). Killick (1990) stresses the importance of continuous incremental policy adjustment which has mutually reinforcing economic and political advantages.

The character and commitment of the political leadership in major adjustment policy are stressed by Nelson (1989). Since there have usually been deep divisions among the strategic elites which determine policy, the skills of the political leaders in achieving consensus have often been a key factor. Martin (1991) stresses the complex and unwieldy top policy-making structures in Nigeria and Zambia (especially the political parties, cabinet, parliament, ministries, central banks), with ministers and officials often ill co-ordinated. This poses problems for the leadership even if the state is autonomous with respect to societal pressures and interests.

Finally, on the balance of societal interests and pressures on state policy, more recent perceptions seem to have changed from the earlier society-centred thesis. Recent case-study work (Mosley *et al.*, 1991; Herbst, 1989; Skalnes, 1989; Grindle and Thomas, 1989) suggests that societal constraints on policy change are not so overwhelming, especially in economic crisis situations. Thus for Grindle and Thomas (1989:221):

> the cases suggest that policy elites can provide initiation, orientation, leadership, ideology, expertise and political sensitivity to major issues of reform. None of these contributions is easily predicted from society centred approaches to understanding public policy.

This perception is also consistent with the prevailing view among political scientists and sociologists that civil society is poorly developed in all but a minority of African countries.

Shams (1989), in a comparison of political experience in Mauritius and Kenya, suggests that adjustment policy must converge with the interests of the groups making up the government if it is to succeed. Clientelism exists in both countries and gives them reasonable stability. This has been inimical to structural adjustment in Kenya but not in Mauritius. Yet his conclusion is that clientelist systems do not necessarily obstruct the implementation of adjustment policies.

In a recent contribution Bates (1988) believes some policy reform is due to fiscal stringency which limits the scope for continuing subsidy policy and underpricing. Further policy reform is seen to be constrained by the difficulty of state elites in anticipating the precise societal effects of policy change and in communicating and persuading powerful interests of the 'national' case for change, especially as he sees no member of a coalition as willing to withdraw its advocacy of the status quo unilaterally. This is a view shared by Callaghy (1990). For Bates the sustainability of policy reform lies with a change in the dominant coalition of workers, industrialists and government which would bring in agricultural (especially export) and consumer interests more centrally.

The sustainability of reform will depend on how quickly the changed policies benefit *new* groups in society, and whether their support can be effectively exploited to balance those who lose from the changes. On this Mosley *et al.* (1991:174-7) take the view that policy change, especially liberalisation, should have increased the political leverage of the beneficiary groups - i.e. the exporting industrialists, large farmers, non-protected borrowers - but that it did not do so because a common interest in reform was not translated into collective action. Often this was because they were politically favoured ethnic groups or groups which were scattered over large areas. Policy instruments where technocrats had a more dominant influence - stabilisation rather than structural and institutional reform - tended to be used more sustainably.

Part II
Summary and Conclusions

In conclusion let us attempt a summary picture of the main actors, processes and influences affecting policy formation in the 1970s and policy change in the 1980s in sub-Saharan Africa, in the light of this review of the literature. The main *actors* in policy-making were state elites in which the political leadership - in some cases a single autocrat and in others a small oligarchy - was dominant. The senior echelons of the bureaucracy, with few exceptions, have played a weak role, lacking adequate dialogue with the political leaders, lacking independence and providing limited technical analysis of policy options. Legislatures have become instruments of the ruling elite, in most cases co-opted or appointed by the political leaders and lacking any independence to influence, scrutinise, debate or approve policy actions. The role of elected representatives in single-party systems has been to lobby for public resources for their constituencies rather than to influence the choice of national policy or regime. Electoral expediency has also required this. The power of the political party as a strategy- or policy-making institution, in largely one-party states, has shifted to the ruling oligarchy or the President. Members of these parties do not seem to have engaged in policy debate or initiative, while grassroots party organisations have not been fostered and used as sounding boards for policy-making.

The exclusive single-party apparatus has served to limit wider political participation in policy determination. Independent ethnic and kinship associations and interest groups have either been abolished, suppressed or channelled through the party, where their influence has been on the distribution of public expenditure and services, not on economic policy determination. Modern interest groups cutting across ethnic and regional divisions, such as business and professional associations and trade unions, do not seem to have played a significant role in forming public policy positions, at least not through open lobbying. Business groups have been heterogeneous in their interests, and lacking in unity on policy perspectives. Their public influence has been weak, and individual businesses seem to have worked more informally by stealth to seek special privileges and exceptions, modifications and delays in the application of policies for themselves. The existence of minority ethnic or foreign interests and the rather 'state-nurtured and protected' nature of indigenous business may partly explain this. Trade unions have generally been a weak influence in Africa, sometimes because the leadership had been suppressed or co-opted. The larger farmers, especially those with political connections, have often been a powerful influence on policy for agriculture and stabilisation. The small farmers appear to have had little influence on government policy.

The *process* of policy formation seems best understood from a state-centred perspective rather than from a society-centred, pluralist one. The apparently 'irrational' economic policies of the 1970s seem to be partly explained by the following features of this process. First, policies have been made in small exclusive political circles. Divisions and debate on policy have been confined to political factions, with little consultation of societal interests or public debate and limited feedback on how policies were working, due to lack of interest or the suppression of societal opinion or scrutiny. Limited attention was paid to compromise and consensus in drawing up proposals for policy change. Policy agendas were narrow and sometimes unrealistically ambitious. Second, the most powerful influence seems to have been the search for political legitimacy and support among influential groups through a patronage and clientelist process rather than through open, politically competitive electoral systems for deciding policies and determining access to state power. This process usually generated policies which were unfavourable to growth, to reduced inequality or to timely economic adjustment. *Inter alia*, it favoured a strategy of administrative and hence political intervention in the allocation of resources, an emphasis on the distribution of state resources rather than on wealth creation, and the creation of offices, institutions and appointments favouring the interests of certain privileged support groups, and not efficient management. There were strong ethnic and regional pressures in the distribution of public resources. The fear of undermining support from privileged and protected groups appears to have impeded necessary changes in economic policy till the mid-1980s.

A third but weaker influence on policy was the regime's ideology, including socialist, populist or market capitalist preferences. However, these have been largely swamped by more systematic 'statist' tendencies throughout Africa since the 1960s. A major feature has been the apparent unresponsiveness of regimes to the modification or reversal of strategies or policies which proved ineffective in economic terms in the 1970s and early 1980s. The main explanation of this situation has been the largely personal, authoritarian, patrimonial nature of regimes which have not been made politically accountable by competitive selection or electoral systems and which have clung to policies favouring and protecting their supporting interest groups.

The timing and scope of economic reform in the 1980s were determined by African regimes themselves, though the content of the reforms was greatly influenced by the pressures and technical analysis of the external financing agencies. The domestic impetus to delayed economic reforms is most frequently explained by the perceived 'crisis' and the threat to the survival of the political regimes. That state elites 'learned from past mistakes' and reversed their earlier ideologies is not yet well established; nor is the notion that authoritarian regimes were more decisive in dealing with economic crisis, stabilisation and adjustment. Decisive and broad policy change seems to depend more on the executive being able to command support and organise coalitions or key support groups; this is ultimately a function of political skill. Consultation by elections or referenda has generally tended to reduce the authority of regimes, admittedly in situations of crisis, and to delay adjustment. The degree of autonomy of state authorities has emerged as stronger than was expected in the early 1980s. The two countries - Botswana and Mauritius - with multi-party systems achieved continuous adjustment to changing economic conditions over time. However, few are willing to generalise from these somewhat special cases, though they both demonstrated a rare political culture of consensus seeking and flexible policy-making.

Part III

Democracy, Development and Adjustment in Developing Countries

6
Democracy and Development: the Debate and Comparative Evidence

The survey of the literature on political change and policy formation in sub-Saharan Africa in Part II throws limited light on whether more openly accountable or pluralist systems achieved, or might have achieved, more effective economic management. The African trend towards authoritarian, monolithic, rule has not been accompanied by better economic policies or performance; quite the reverse. On the other hand, there have been too few cases of politically competitive and liberal economies in Africa to establish what might have been the situation under African geographical, economic and cultural conditions. Before examining the prospects for political and economic change in Africa we first look at wider developing country experience in a review of the literature on the systematic relationship between political regime type and (a) economic growth and development in this chapter, and (b) policies for adjustment, especially under 'crisis' conditions, in Chapter 7.

The nature of the debate

For over two decades the debate about the relationship between democracy and economic and social performance has drawn on empirical (including quantitative) research to test its hypotheses. The literature is extensive but two recent publications provide a helpful summary and critical evaluation. Nelson (1987) reviews the evolution of thinking on political participation, while Sirowy and Inkeles (1990) comprehensively and critically review the cross-sectional quantitative evidence amassed so far, which tests the extent of the association between political regime type (the degree of polyarchy) and economic growth and inequality. Before examining the main empirical conclusions we briefly review and evaluate the theoretical perspectives of the last 25 years and the hypotheses and arguments deployed.

To a large extent the debate seems to have been conducted in terms of 'compatibility' and 'conflict' perspectives. On the one hand, there are those who see political participation and democratic systems and economic and social development as mutually reinforcing. On the other hand, there are those who consider that democratic politics and procedures hinder economic development. Some have looked to authoritarian regimes to encourage stabilisation and economic growth and even to reduce inequality. One variant of the incompatibility thesis is that democracy may eventually accompany development at a certain level, but the process of rapid modernisation can make its introduction premature. In addition to these two major categories there are those who take an agnostic position on the relationship and who believe that factors other than the nature of the political regime are the dominant influence on the economic prospects for developing countries.

In this debate the nature of democracy is not always clearly specified but the key political features under exploration usually centre on the extent to which the system or the specific regimes are 'inclusive' or 'exclusive' in their approach - seeking to activate, or not, a wide range of voices in national politics. The conceptual basis for distinguishing systems in terms of political democracy rests ultimately on the extent to which political elites are selected by the citizens via regular and meaningful elections, and this in turn centres on the degree of freedom of association and speech and the competitiveness of the electoral system.[18]

The theorising on the effects of different political institutions or regimes on economic and social development is not always as precise as it should be. The links or processes are not always spelt out. We examine them here under the following categories: (i) modernisation, political stability, and growth; (ii) politics and markets; and (iii) the efficiency of state decision-making: (a) decisiveness and rationality, (b) a 'firm hand': policies on investment and saving, and (c) egalitarianism: public expenditure patterns.

We shall first consider in turn these specific elements and the respective empirical evidence/research bearing on each of them. This

---

[18] See Bollen (1980), and Bollen and Grandjean (1981), for a thorough exploration of the concept of political democracy and its measurement. Bollen compares the theoretical definitions and previous measures of political democracy. He develops an index which seeks to measure two main features: 'popular sovereignty' and 'political liberties'. The former includes three measures: fairness of elections, executive selection and legislative selection. The latter uses indicators of press freedom, freedom of group opposition and government sanctions.

is followed by a brief review of the empirical evidence on research relating democracy and economic growth *outcomes*, and then an evaluation of the current state of the debate.

Modernisation, political stability and economic growth

Modernisation theorists writing in the 1960s were initially concerned with the social-economic conditions which would enable newly independent states in Africa and Asia to develop stable and democratic political structures. According to Coleman (1971), there were a number of functional pre-requisites for democratic development: these included a high level of urbanisation, widespread literacy, relatively high *per capita* incomes, geographical and social mobility, a high degree of commercialisation and industrialisation, an extensive mass communications network, and widespread participation in modern social and economic processes. Others believed that a social consensus was required, or a civic culture which encouraged the spread of democratic values (Lipset, 1959).

Against this, Rustow (1970) was of the opinion that a search for functional pre-requisites conflated the process of democratisation, without providing an insight into the various phases of democratic development. He maintained that national unity provided the starting point for this development, which evolves through a prolonged period of political struggle before agreement is reached on rules and procedures and a consensus develops over the desirability of resolving conflict through negotiation.

Huntington (1965) argued against a 'premature' move to competitive multi-party politics in traditional but early modernising societies in Asia, Latin America and Africa. His argument was dynamic, and focused on the tension between the growth of social pressures and divisive conflicts, and whether they could be matched fast enough by the development of political institutions to handle and reconcile them in the 'public interest'. In societies which are basically heterogeneous, rapid urbanisation, increased literacy, better education, improved communications and newly organised economic interests were seen by Huntington to generate increased political mobilisation, greater participation and higher aspirations on the part of sectional interests, all of which had to be reconciled if political stability and order were to be maintained. Geertz (1963) believed that 'primordial loyalties' based on kinship, religion, language and culture would undermine efforts to build a durable political system in modernising societies. In his view, these traditional loyalties would inevitably come into conflict with 'modern' civic values in transitional states, giving rise to problems of 'tribalism' and 'communalism' which would impede the process of national integration.

Concerns about the potentially disruptive effects of modernisation gave rise to an interest in political institution-building. Huntington emphasised the integrative role of modern political institutions, especially political parties, in fostering participation, and in providing the state with a source of legitimacy and authority in order to guard against institutional decay. In his view, institutionalisation is more effectively achieved if (a) competition between political elites is minimised in order to avoid factionalism; (b) multi-party systems are discouraged and single parties encouraged to economise on limited talent; and (c) pressures on bureaucracies are reduced in order to limit corruption. Political instability and disorder decrease as a result, thereby assisting both political and economic development.

Other writers were concerned with the integrative role that could be played by functional interest groups in the process of political modernisation (Almond and Coleman, 1971). A different view was that modernising elites played a key role in disseminating modern political values to the traditional mass of the population, to serve as the basis for national integration and political modernisation (Binder, 1965).

In view of the problems associated with efforts to create democratic institutions, writers such as Apter (1965) saw authoritarianism as the most appropriate means of overcoming societal heterogeneity, conflict and discontent, at least in the early stage of development, in order to forge unity and consensus. A variant on this theme was the view that military-authoritarian rather than civil rule was most favourable to modernisation, stability and growth because of the disciplined outlook, the power to impose law and order, and the autonomy to introduce effective policies and avoid the need for wide consultation and political participation (O'Brien, 1979).

Huntington and others were writing over twenty years ago, but a contemporary observer of African politics (Callaghy, 1986) has since elaborated some of their arguments. The ideology of development (which asserts that the development of the country is the highest goal of government) poses a serious threat to political democracy. Because expectations are high, frustrations arise among modernising elites especially the military who then intervene in politics and weaken the already fragile and limited experience of democracy. A cycle of military intervention is established in the name of legitimate development and justice, which then undermines the institutionalisation of democracy and ultimately development as well. What is the empirical evidence on the relationship between instability, political participation and economic performance?

First, does political instability hinder economic growth? Of course, at a basic level economic development requires reasonable peace, law and order, and authority to enforce contracts and to permit the functioning of markets, trade, production and investment. Kuznets saw an unmistakable association between economic performance, stability and political structure. In a major empirical work he concluded (1966:453):

> Political instability, and non-representativeness of the regime combined with an authoritarian structure dominated by personalist leaders and backed by familiar and ethnic ties and police are hardly favourable conditions for economic growth - even in the early phases of transition from traditional pre-modern economic society.

More recently McGowan and Johnson (1985) offer some empirical evidence from Africa in the 1956-84 period to show that instability, in the sense of frequent changes of regimes (including coup d'états and military intervention), above a certain critical level inhibits economic activity. Barro (1991) found a negative relationship between political instability (revolutions, coups and political assassinations) and economic growth and investment for a larger and wider sample of countries over the period 1960-85. He interprets this instability as operating via property rights on private investment but recognises that his correlation could reflect a political response to bad economic outcomes.

Second, does greater participation and more open politics endanger stability and coherence as Huntington and others seem to imply? Stability depends not only on participation but even more on regime *response*. Politically accountable regimes have tended to be more moderate in their response and are less likely to repress dissent and induce a violent response. Electoral participation is not associated with instability and political violence, though research has found little difference in the level of conflict between developing countries with democratic and non-democratic institutions (Nelson, 1987). In retrospect, Huntington's early insight into the need for political institutions and procedures to keep pace with the pressures for participation so that these can be channelled and tamed, over-emphasised their strength and potential, at least in Africa (Zolberg, 1968). Thus the experience has been more of self-interested state elites which often have shown little interest in promoting participation or economic development.

While single-party and centralised regimes have usually encompassed some ethnic and regional interests, they have tended to exclude the full range, including the more modern interest groups, and thus have endangered stability (Rothchild and Foley, 1988).

Politics and markets

One chain of reasoning sees a link between democracy and growth - sometimes equitable growth - in the form of market systems rather than state-administered economic allocation and activity. There are two elements to this argument. First, there is the relationship between democracy and markets or between political and economic liberalism. There has for some time been a school of thought which sees the two as associated or mutually reinforcing. (e.g. Lipset, 1959; Friedman, 1962 and 1980). Second, there are the implications of market-oriented systems for competition, efficient allocation, innovation and economic growth. The economic literature and research on this area are vast and those who argue for economic liberalism obviously believe the balance of evidence supports a positive relationship.

Lindblom (1977) in a major study of markets and politics makes the following assertions which are highly relevant to the current debate about developing countries:

- Both polyarchy and market systems reflect an underlying struggle for freedom from authority and freedom to trade without arbitrary interference.
- Polyarchy and markets are mutually reinforcing because (a) polyarchic systems have certain rules for constraining rather than mobilising authority (i.e. they protect freedom of contracts, and private property, and hence strengthen market systems), (b) both practise decentralisation in decision taking and diffusion of power and influence, while (c) both recognise man's limited cognitive capacity to organise society and solve social and economic problems centrally and hence point to interactive processes and mutual adjustment as an alternative.
- Political democracy has been unable to exist except coupled with markets. Markets seem to be a necessary but not a sufficient condition for democracy.

Surprisingly there seems to be little empirical work systematically relating political systems to the market orientation of countries. A recent exception is Pourgerami (1988), who finds a positive and statistically significant association between a measure of the market orientation of economies and their degree of political freedom. However, his cross-country comparison for 1984-6 covers both developed and developing countries and he measures human rights records rather than the institutional aspects of democracy.

On the basis of historical experience, however, there does appear to be broad agreement among economic historians and development economists that authoritarian regimes, where command over economic and political resources was relatively undifferentiated, were a major feature of those societies from which market economies emerged. Moreover, in these societies the emergence of capitalism preceded the emergence of democracy (Ruttan, 1991).

Comparative historical experience on the apparent political pre-conditions for successful industrialisation was explored by Holt (1966). He looked at two pairs of countries: China (1644-1911) and Japan (1600-1870); France (1600-1789) and England (1560-1780) during the periods in which industrialisation in China and France lagged behind that of their 'rivals'. The most significant common political features of the slower industrialisers (China and France) were that (a) there was greater central government involvement in resource mobilisation and allocation, (b) central state policy-makers were not subject to institutionalised checks, balances and vetoes, and (c) policy enforcement was more centrally controlled, with more reliable instruments and various techniques for securing (and enforcing) compliance. The greater degree of pre-democratic political checks on central policy-making power and the greater decentralisation of administration and independence of civil society were seen as closely associated with the subsequent superior industrial performance in England and Japan.

North (1984) also brings out the political struggle between the state and the commercial class over clear economic rules (or 'property rights') to reduce uncertainty. He sees as an essential feature of efficient factor and product markets the reduction of the potentially high 'transactions costs' involved in specifying, negotiating and enforcing contracts. The state has a comparative advantage in the provision of such services and the promulgation of moral and political codes of behaviour which lower these costs and facilitate economic activity and growth. However, for North the self-interest of the state elite or rulers lies in maximising revenue or rents through the exercise of its monopoly power. A mutually beneficial outcome results only from the state 'trading' the provision of the above services for revenue. It has to be challenged to do so by the political development of countervailing power from the commercial class - an earlier stage than polyarchy or democracy.

Historically in Europe, representative bodies were created in order to exchange revenues for commercial freedom and economic rights. In England, after a long struggle, parliament had won these rights against the King by the seventeenth century and capital markets subsequently developed to form the basis of the industrial revolution. According to North England's successful political struggle for economic freedom distinguishes its subsequent economic development from that of Spain where the monarch was able to resist pressures for widening political representation.

On the basis of this type of evidence some scholars (e.g. Lipset and Huntington) consider that democracy must wait for the development of an independent and robust bourgeoisie or capitalist class. More recently Hyden (1983) somewhat controversially considers sub-Saharan Africa as still predominantly pre-capitalist in its attitudes and argues that a more independent capitalist class and market economy must evolve and need to be encouraged before democratic movement can be expected. In this case democracy becomes conditional on the emergence of an independent capitalist class operating in a market economy, rather than being a stimulus for capitalist economic growth (cf. Schumpeter, 1976).

Diamond (1988:69) brings out the precariousness of a democratic culture in the African context where the indigenous capitalist class desperately depends on access to state power and resources:

> Democracy requires moderation and restraint. It demands not only that people care about political competition but also that they not care too much; that their emotional and tangible stake in its outcome not be so great that they cannot contemplate defeat. In Nigeria and throughout much of Africa, the swollen state has turned politics into a zero-sum game in which everything of value is at stake in an election, and hence candidates, communities and parties feel compelled to win at any cost.

A context where politics is a matter of 'life and death' is unfavourable not only to democracy or democratisation; it is also unfavourable to development, because access to, and manipulation of, the government spending process replaces productive economic activity by entrepreneurs.

More recently the 'new political economy' or 'public choice' school sees politics as characterised by a plethora of special interest groups competing for access to the benefits and resources that can be allocated by government via lobbying and voting. Public policy then reflects the existence of distributional coalitions in society which seek subsidies, transfers, protected positions and monopoly access to resources - usually termed 'rent seeking'. The upshot is 'distortions' in the functioning of competitive markets, loss of economic welfare and impediments to growth, not just from misallocation but also from the wasteful cost of the rent-seeking activities themselves. For this school, 'rational' politics leads to 'irrational' economic policies.

These hypotheses have been applied to the Third World but their general validity, and in particular the extent of their application to developing countries, is still disputed. It should be added that 'public choice' analysts would not necessarily attribute the main factor in such irrational economic outcomes to basically democratic political systems but rather to the pure self-interest of all individuals including those who constitute the 'state'. The survival of rulers under closed authoritarian systems can generate similar types of 'rent seeking' and market distortion by their need to survive in power (see Chapter 4). Adherents of the public choice school would see the size of the state and its power and resources as the key to this type of political pressure and economic outcome. It is less clear (and an area for future exploration) how far the 'strength' and size of the state (which has grown fairly systematically and steadily in developing countries) are related to the type of regime and whether authoritarian regimes are more or less likely than more open democratic ones to limit the scope for markets.

There has been growing interest in measuring the effect of the size of the public sector on economic growth (see Landau, 1986; Easterly and Witzel, 1989 for recent reviews). State size measured by indicators such as government consumption and expenditure as a share of GDP seems to be negatively correlated with growth, while government revenues and taxation yield conflicting results. So far it has not been possible to measure the government's degree of regulation of the national economy on a comparative basis.

Possible hypotheses are that the greater the scale of state involvement in an economy, the more difficulties are posed for economic management and performance by either a more open democratic system of government or its opposite. Empirically the link between democracy and growth via state size has not yet been established. Weede (1983) found that the subset of his democratic countries with large state sectors performed worse than those with smaller sectors, but Marsh (1988) showed that this effect arose from the former's high level of development. More empirical work relating political systems to types and scales of state involvement is needed. So far only public investment seems to be correlated significantly and positively with democracy and negatively with growth. The long-term relationship of public consumption, revenue, taxation and budget deficits to political regime remains unclear and no work has been done to relate measured price distortions in economies to political variables (Landau, 1986).

Finally, there is a substantial body of opinion that holds that rural development and successful agrarian reform are dependent on decentralisation, widespread participation and diffused political support, even if strong central political commitment is necessary to initiate such reform. According to this view, many states which initiate reforms paradoxically see the ultimate diffusion of participation and power as a serious threat and fear their loss of control over the development of powerful local interest groups which are the pre-condition for sustaining rural development (Rondinelli, 1986). It has also been argued that the existence of competitive elections, as well as the institutionalisation of political participation, induces state policies and bureaucracies to be more responsive to the needs of rural people, which has often been the key not only to greater economic development but also to less inequality (for Asia see King, 1981; and for an African example see Harvey and Lewis, 1990).

Efficient state decision-making

The major channels by which different types of political rule are seen to influence economic performance concern the quality and strength of state economic policy decisions, in particular those affecting saving and investment, inflation, and resource allocation, all of which bear on growth of output.

Decisiveness and consistency

A common argument in favour of authoritarian rule is that there is an overriding need - especially in the early stages of development - to ensure strong and decisive state policy intervention. This is seen as essential in order to respond to excessive expectations and demands on available resources, to reconcile conflicting pressures and to avoid paralysed decision-making or inconsistent policies - all of which are seen as the likely adverse features of highly pluralist and participatory political systems.

Against this, it has been argued that democratic regimes have not had a monopoly of inconsistent policies; authoritarian regimes have vacillated; and even in regimes with a narrow participatory base and small policy circles, factional and ideological disputes can paralyse action as much as those with highly mobilised broad participation (Nelson 1987, 1990).

Indeed, there are some who take the view that, with more representative and responsive state institutions and greater freedom of association and communication among citizens, there will be more airing of policy options, more extensive consultation and feedback from a wide range of interests *before* government policy is made. Policy formation is thus likely to be more workable, credible and predictable and less likely to constrain rather than encourage entrepreneurial activity (Killick, 1990).

Recent evaluations of authoritarian rule in Africa bring out the damaging economic consequences of personal and patrimonial styles of governance. Authoritarian rule in post-colonial Africa has been associated with fairly widespread and systemic economic stagnation and decline which does not seem to have been parallelled to the same extent elsewhere in the Third World (Sandbrook, 1985).

The more representative the regime the greater the legitimacy it has for its decisions. The link between the political legitimacy of democratic regimes and their economic performance is brought out by Diamond, Linz and Lipset (1988). They argue that historically the more successful a regime is at providing what people want the greater and more deeply rooted tends to be its legitimacy. A long record of successful political and economic performance helps to build a large reservoir of legitimacy which helps the system to endure crises and challenges better. Conversely, regimes with low political legitimacy find it difficult to perform effectively in maintaining civil order, personal security, and the adjudication of conflicts and in maintaining predictability in making and implementing the decisions on which economic and social performance depends. Though cautioning against deterministic links, they nevertheless see a clear link between the economic performance of democratic regimes and the probability of their survival.

The 'firm hand': saving and investment

One of the most venerable and frequent arguments deployed in favour of authoritarian rather than democratic rule concerns the propensity of a society to limit its consumption in order to ensure adequate resources for investment. This persistent theme in the writing of political scientists is consistent not only with the importance which the theories of economists attach to investment but also with the empirical evidence which has fairly consistently traced the scale of capital formation as an influence on economic growth.

The political theories seem to focus mainly on the notion that democratic regimes, unlike authoritarian ones, are more preoccupied with distributional issues and lack the firmness (a) to shift income towards the richer sections of the population which are considered to have higher propensities to save or (b) to ensure a degree of restraint on consumption (e.g. Weede, 1983).

The political science literature has a notion of 'forcing' savings which seems at odds with, or unaware of, economic research on the policy determinants of private savings. These focus on the encouragement of financial asset holding and the extension of savings-mobilising institutions', positive real interest rates and indirect rather than direct control over credit creation (Deaton, 1990). Nor is there much awareness that there is no evidence that savings are positively related to income inequality nor that income inequality leads to higher growth (World Bank, 1990b).

Indeed, only nodding acquaintance with financial policy in Third World countries in the last two decades shows that many governments, and specifically their public sectors, have failed to save their revenues and incomes, whether they were authoritarian or democratic, and that most of them followed policies of 'financial repression' which discouraged the mobilisation of private savings by the banks and other financial institutions. In any case there seems to have been little or no exploration of how different types of political regime are, or were, *expected* to influence saving, nor to evaluate how far they succeeded, if at all, in practice. A coherent theory of the respective roles of representative versus authoritarian systems needs to explore alternative policy instruments and objectives which political rulers are supposed to use to influence saving.

Investment rates are another matter, but the curious thing is that most political science quantitative assessments of the effects of democracy on growth *abstract* from the effects of investment rates on growth in trying to isolate the influence of political variables. Yet their own theories point to levels of investment and saving as one of the key channels for the influences of authoritarian rule on economic performance (Sirowy and Inkeles, 1990).

A variant of the saving/investment thesis by O'Donnell (1979) enjoyed considerable discussion in the late 1970s. His thesis relates to the different types of political regime that appear to be necessary for different stages of industrialisation. Based to a large extent on Latin American experience, it is a theory of historical transition. The initial phase of industrialisation centred on the development of consumer goods industries via import substitution is postulated to thrive on inclusive 'populist' democratic regimes. However, the later phase of industrialisation involves intermediate and capital goods and is more demanding technologically, managerially and in flows of foreign capital. This phase is seen to require political regimes which attempt more austere economic policies, which resist populist pressures and strikes, limit inflation, and minimise balance-of-payments deficits and debt in order to attract the necessary foreign capital and maintain competitiveness. Popular participation is thus seen as an obstacle to a more advanced stage of industrialisation and growth. The recipe is seen to be repression and professionalism in the form of an authoritarian regime with a technocratic bureaucracy.

There has been much exploration of this thesis in the light of experience but the balance of opinion has not found it convincing. Economic transformation and dynamic growth occurred under democratic systems in Latin America (e.g. Brazil 1968-74), and obstacles to growth arose in the absence of competitive electoral processes (Collier, 1979a).

A more modern variant of the savings/investment argument focuses on the pressures on the use and management of state resources in an open democratic system. The argument is used by Bardhan (1984) to account for slow and slowing economic growth in the 1970s in the world's largest democracy - India. Bardhan sees the Indian state as a loose and uneasy coalition of propertied interests, industrial, agricultural and professional, which have to be placated by the provision of jobs, subsidies and grants from state revenues. With state resources and jobs allocated on the basis of political clientelism, public sector resources for capital formation are eroded; effective management and efficient allocation of state resources are undermined.

Although the democratic system is not at the centre of Bardhan's perceived process, it is seen as facilitating it. Democracy has survived in India perhaps because there has been considerable diversity, with no single dominant class or interest and a vibrant civil society. In the early years the Congress system provided a resilient mechanism for conflict management: the distribution of spoils in exchange for political support. This was a centralised organisation responsive to pressures from important interest groups, with institutionalised procedures for doing deals which lent a degree of legitimacy and moderation, absorbing dissent and co-opting leaders from the subordinate classes (Manor, 1981 and 1983). However, democracy has encouraged a proliferation of demands for spoils in this pluralist system. This, in turn, has reduced the resources available for public investment and their efficient use, as well as the more protected and feather-bedded activities in the private sector in response to rent-seeking. As growth slows it feeds back into fiscal crisis and political insecurity, thus worsening the prospects (Bardhan, 1984).

The striking thing about Bardhan's thesis is that it has been closely paralleled by analysts for other regions and societies where democracy has not effectively existed. Bates' (1981) analysis for Africa as a whole, Barkan (1984) for Kenya and Joseph (1985) for Nigeria point to a similar nexus in which authoritarian rulers and regimes seek political support via patronage with similar adverse effects on budgets, resource allocation and jobs, and a self-defeating outcome (see Chapter 5).

Any analysis which explores the effect of democracy on development needs to disentangle the lobbying and responses to various legitimate interests in the polity from those which might be considered illegitimate and excessive. The heart of the debate lies in the way different pressures and conflicts are handled under 'representative' as opposed to 'non-representative' political systems and their implications for public resource use. This seems to be lacking in the literature.

Egalitarian orientation: patterns of public expenditure and policy

There is an expectation among scholars that the more democratic the regime the more 'distributive' or egalitarian will be the orientation of its policies. This is not expected of authoritarian regimes, in particular 'bureaucratic' or 'military' as opposed to socialist regimes. The need to be responsive to a wider range of domestic interests (in order to win votes and political support), including the poorer sections of society and their basic needs, suggests a greater policy emphasis in democracy on rural development including agrarian reform, with greater opportunities for local participation, policies for smallholders and small entrepreneurs, greater health and education expenditures especially at the primary level, and more progressive taxation, charging and transfer systems.

There are surprisingly few comparative studies of differences in specific *policy inputs* (e.g. budget control, public expenditure behaviour, pricing policy) and/or *policy outputs* such as quality of life indicators (literacy, mortality, etc.), which relate them to political regime type (Sirowy and Inkeles, 1990). An exception is Sloan and Tedin's 1987 study of 20 Latin American countries using annual data (where available) for the period 1960-80, which looked at a mixture of policy inputs and outputs. Democratic regimes did not systematically perform in line with scholarly expectations. Though they demonstrated a relatively good record on health expenditures and health indicators, they did not do so on education. As regards Africa a comparative study by Berg-Schlosser (1984) showed only average levels of health and education expenditures for democratic regimes, but the lowest defence expenditures. Socialist regimes performed best on education, health and improvements in measures of the quality of life between 1960 and 1975. In Nigeria in periods of civilian democratic rule, Bienen (1985) established that, despite populist leaders, there was no pressure from below for policies to deal with personal income redistribution. Distribution issues were communally or ethnically defined and centred on the allocation of revenues from the federal government to the regional states, under both democratic and authoritarian regimes. Williamson and Pampel (1986), from a sample of 32 developing countries, found that the level of political democracy did not seem to facilitate social security programmes, although it did so in a sample of industrialised countries. This was seen as supporting the thesis that democracy will only affect the distribution of societal resources at high levels of income where a 'surplus' can be more easily extracted for this purpose.

Some of those who have studied disaster prevention in developing countries believe that it is no accident that the countries that have been most successful in famine prevention in the recent past have typically had relatively pluralistic politics with open channels of communication for criticism (Drèze and Sen, 1991:18). Most warnings of imminent dangers have tended to come from general reports of floods, droughts or economic dislocation through the press or political opposition, drawing the attention of the authorities to the need for urgent action. India and Botswana have been compared favourably with China from this point of view (Sen, 1983). However, a more systematic inter-country comparison would be needed to establish this plausible hypothesis.

The greater equity or basic-needs orientation of democratic regimes in the Third World remains uncorroborated by the limited evidence so far. There is a strong case for more comparative research which measures the expenditure and revenue-raising patterns suggested above, and quality of life indicators which are becoming more readily available (see UNDP, 1991).

Quantitative research

Democracy and income distribution

Looking at *outcomes* rather than policy inputs, Sirowy and Inkeles (1990) have reviewed 12 studies relating measures of democracy to indicators of the distribution of income across countries. Seven yield a qualified inverse relationship between democracy and inequality and the rest show either an inverse or no significant relationship. Hence there is no robust confirmation of the thesis of several scholars that political democracy (when measured at a point in time) is associated with greater equality. However, the evidence seems to permit the conclusion that political democracy does not widely exacerbate inequality, net of other influences.

Democracy and economic growth

Studies in the 1950s and 1960s attempted to establish a statistical association between indicators of political and economic development. Three major generalisations emerged from this body of research according to Ruttan (1991): (i) low-income newly independent countries, characterised by low levels of political institutionalisation, low institutional density, political instability and violence, had low rates of growth - both total and *per capita*; (ii) low-income countries with authoritarian political systems experienced more rapid rates of economic growth than countries with more democratic political systems; and (iii) at higher levels of *per capita* income ($750 in 1985 prices) this positive relationship tended to disappear.

Research in the 1970s and 1980s attempted to construct more complex models that measured elements in different types of political rule and their influence on growth, but controlled to some extent for other systematic influences. Sirowy and Inkeles (1990) reviewed nineteen cross-national quantitative studies, all of which covered developing countries, though a few also included developed countries in their sample. Six of these nineteen studies focused on differences between military and civilian regimes rather than democratic versus undemocratic ones. Their findings were fairly inconclusive though civilian regimes may on balance have been better at improving the basic quality of life of the citizenry and improving the distribution of access to health and school facilities.

As regards *Africa*, Ravenhill (1980) has made a comparative study of civilian and military regimes over the period from 1960 (representing independence) to 1973 (before the major oil price shock) and distinguished between established, civilian regimes, military regimes and alternating military and civil regimes (see Chapter 3). Performance was measured by real GDP growth and 'intermediary' variables, such as gross investment, exports and reserves, food prices. No really key economic policy variables were included and only primary school enrolment and military expenditure were used as policy tests, with no measure of the distributional aspects of regimes' performance.

The results showed no significant relationship between regime type and economic performance. Among matched pairs no regime type performed better overall, though the Ghanaian military regime of 1966-9 recorded a much lower performance than its civilian successors and predecessors. Ravenhill questioned whether a distinction between military and civilian regimes is very meaningful or fruitful because it is not clear that the style or the process of politics itself in a military regime is necessarily different from civilian rule, at least in its authoritarian variant.

Thirteen studies, based on democratic versus undemocratic political systems, measure performance by economic growth, sometimes by quality of life indices, and occasionally by policy measures such as government social expenditure or intermediate variables like exports. Only one of these (Berg Schlosser, 1984) is based on sub-Saharan African experience alone; it is interesting for its use of a four-category political typology, reviewed in Chapter 3. The performance of these four types was measured over those periods when the regime characteristics did not change substantially. Only 15 out of 45 African countries were 'stable' for 10 years during the period of 1960-80 and 6 of these were 'polyarchic'. The performance indicators included growth of GNP *per capita*, a quality of life index, and selected measures of public expenditure allocation (e.g. education, health and defence). Berg-Schlosser's correlations and conclusions for the period were that unstable countries (more than half) scored low on both economic growth and trends in egalitarianism, as did military regimes; the stable socialist countries had low growth but were more egalitarian over time than the stable authoritarian regimes. The latter had the highest growth but were poor performers on measures of 'disparity reduction'. The stable democratic/polyarchic countries performed moderately on both growth and reduction of inequality reduction.

The importance of instability in performance emerges clearly. But Berg-Schlosser's other conclusions must be treated with some caution. His sample of countries in each regime category did not seem adequate to support his firm judgements on differential performance and his measures of inequality seemed rather limited.

In *developing countries as a whole*, of thirteen studies which related democracy and growth performance, three reported findings showing unqualified negative effect of democracy on rates of growth. Six reported no relationship and four suggested a qualified or conditional relationship. Hence, the outcome of this work is inconclusive according to Sirowy and Inkeles (1990).

The inconclusiveness of this mainly cross-sectional statistical work is not really surprising because of the methodological and data problems involved which need to be resolved if further work in this field is to prove useful (see Bollen, 1980; Bollen and Grandjean, 1981; and Sirowy and Inkeles, 1990 for a thorough discussion). The main issues are the following. First, there is the problem of the political typology and its measurement. This has centred largely on the political party structure, the regularity and meaningfulness (competitiveness, etc.) of elections, and the extent of political freedom. Some studies use ordinal and some cardinal ranking, and the weighting of different elements in their index is usually obscure. Further refinement here suggests more effort to assess or measure the institutions and mechanisms for consultation, and the degrees of 'openness', in states and political systems which are not basically liberal-democratic (see Chapter 5). As Nelson (1987) points out, there are not likely to be any universal relationships and the implications for growth and income distribution are likely to depend on the *degree and kind* of political participation.

Second, there are weaknesses in the specification of the economic growth models. Few use 'controls' for factors which are known to affect growth (e.g. the initial level of economic development, human capital levels, the size of the public sector) but are unlikely to reflect differences in regime characteristics. This may reflect the lack of co-operative work between economists and political scientists and the lack of awareness of each other's work and current perceptions.

Third, there remain severe data problems. Too many of the studies use political data relating to the pre-1970s. There is a shortage and lack of comparability of data for measuring inequality. Time periods (point of time measurement and time lags involved in the likely impact of political variables on economic and social outcomes) are especially difficult to resolve. In particular they pose the danger that, in allowing for changes in the type of regime over time, the analyst ends up measuring political *stability* rather than the nature of governance especially as they are often so closely correlated in practice.

Finally, and perhaps most significant of all, much of this empirical work has focused on the implications of political regime type for economic and social *outcomes*. Yet the 'links' or intermediary mechanisms often remain unclear, unspecified and untested. As our earlier discussion showed, the main channels by which more or less democratic rule might influence growth and equality are via the influence of the state on stability, predictability of economic and social policy and its implementation, resource allocation mechanisms, public revenue and expenditure behaviour, etc. Yet, with the exception of more recent empirical research on stabilisation and adjustment (see Chapter 7) little systematic work has been done on the specific *policy* outcomes of different political regimes and institutions.

7
Democracy, Adjustment Policy and Economic Crisis

After our review of systematic long-run relationships between democracy and economic and social performance, we now turn to the literature on the politics of economic adjustment. This is a literature about policy decision-making rather than outcomes. One aspect concerns policies of what might be termed 'continuous adjustment' or adaptation to changing economic conditions and opportunities, which is a vital condition for economic growth. The literature on this is mainly centred on the political economy of individual countries and our interest here is in political explanations of those economies - mainly East Asian - which were flexible and dynamic over a long period.

The second aspect is the politics of stabilisation and structural reform under 'crisis' conditions partly because of sudden and substantial changes in international conditions at the end of the 1970s, but also because of the lack of past 'continuous adjustment' by many countries. Since these economic challenges in the 1980s have been accompanied, or preceded, by transition to political liberalisation and democratisation, especially in Latin America, political scientists have explored the implications of these for adjustment.

The politics of continuous adjustment

A number of countries achieved flexible and adaptable policies during the 1970s and 1980s, promoting trade with the world economy, controlling inflation, raising savings and maintaining growth despite major change in world financial and product markets. These include Taiwan, South Korea, Malaysia, Mauritius, as well as, possibly, Indonesia, Chile and Mexico. The features of the political culture and institutions which generate this type of economic behaviour have not been systematically studied though there is a substantial analysis of the political economy of individual countries.

Taiwan and South Korea have been two of the most dynamic economies which have continuously adjusted to changing world conditions over the last 25 years or more, in terms of modulating the impact of foreign competition, promoting exports on competitive world markets, introducing new technologies and industries as international technology and competition patterns change, while at the same time maintaining national competitiveness, prioritising foreign-exchange allocation and encouraging investible saving to help achieve these objectives.

Much of the debate about this performance has focused on two views. One is the neo-classical economist's view that there has been progressive reform towards a free market economy and exploitation of comparative advantage - an open export-oriented strategy maintained in the face of external shocks via timely deflation and exchange-rate adjustment (Balassa, 1989). The other main view attempts to 'explain' successful performance in terms of centrally determined and implemented government strategies. These are seen as selective intervention in markets, plus protection and assistance, combined with no state intervention to protect groups vulnerable to the consequences of market rationality. Both now accept that the means of production are mostly privately owned and profits are privately appropriated by the business groups. The difference centres on the character of the state's role.

Two recent and comprehensive assessments of both Taiwan and Korea are White and Wade (1990), and Wade (1991), who fall into the second camp. For them the dominant political explanation for a successful interventionist strategy has lain with the authoritarian, corporatist state since 1949 in Taiwan and from 1961 in South Korea. They draw attention to three main features in this link. First, both central governments have, at least until quite recently, been concerned to prevent the emergence of independent channels for interest aggregation and articulation. Tight restrictions on association, a positive discouragement of pluralist interests, and an elected legislature with little role in policy-making have therefore given central state policy-makers an unusual degree of autonomy. At the same time, there has been what they term a 'corporatist' alliance between the state leadership, the bureaucracy and business interests, though not labour unions. According to Wade, this allows the state to define national goals and to take unusual powers to enable these goals to be accomplished without having to enter into the bargaining and shifting alliances which have characterised policy-making in the authoritarian regimes of Latin America.

Second, the pre-eminent single-party-dominated executive in both countries has had a clear and urgent ideology of industrialisation, and a comprehensive rather than piecemeal perspective and framework for policy formulation and implementation. For Wade (1991) elected legislatures are less likely to be directed by a view of the common good than by the importunity of partial interests. The industrialisation ideology was generated and sustained in both cases by 'threat' from powerful external enemies (mainland China and North Korea) and therefore owes more to political and cultural history than to political regime type as such. Third, a feature brought out especially for Korea by Luedde-Neurath (1990), was the integrated, military-style organisation of the bureaucracy especially when intervening in innovative or crisis situations. Added to this was the Korean people's tolerance of military-style authority and lack of freedom in the economic and daily life, which is sometimes attributed to Confucian values, but was presumably made more acceptable by steadily rising real wages. The fact that extensive and detailed economic and technological intervention by the state bureaucracy did not lead to a chaos of contradictory regulations and delays in Korea is, according to Luedde-Neurath, due to organisational characteristics like the highly effective channels of communication as well as the good quality of information. Efficient bureaucrats of high status enforced as well as formulated and monitored policies. The bureaucracy was, in turn, overseen by a 'feared' audit. The approach was a pragmatic and flexible one in which policies were reversed and organisations changed or by-passed if they did not work.

This institutional aspect is brought out by others. Haggard, Kim and Moon (1990) point to the institutional reforms launched by the Korean military leadership in the 1950s which purged and reformed the civil service, enhancing the status and power of the technocrats in coherent policy formulation and the quality of the civil servants at lower levels, who implemented the policy. They stress that the switch from import-substitution policies to more export-oriented strategies in the 1960s was made possible by this key administrative change which stemmed from military autocracy. In this lasting transformation the private sector continued to have channels of access to the government but no longer dominated the policy process in typically rent-seeking ways, as it had done in the earlier period when the party, the private sector and the political executive itself had penetrated the administration through patron-client networks.

From the other (neo-classical economic) perspective, the key to Korean and Taiwanese dynamism and adaptability was the market-oriented economy, with its open trading policy, combined with appropriate timing of adjustment of the real exchange rate and conservative fiscal policies. If this school may have underestimated the degree of state intervention and guidance in the markets, it sees the clue to success in effective macroeconomic policies and the degree of freedom that was present in product, labour and capital markets. This school does not seem to take a view on the nature of the political regime type which followed its preferred economic strategy. In these particular cases it was authoritarian and repressive but it is not obvious that this was essential to the policy behaviour.

Crisis and adjustment policy under democratic systems

The 1980s have been a period concerned with economic disequilibria - high inflation, heavy indebtedness, large fiscal and balance-of-payments deficits - which have created 'crises' of stabilisation and structural adjustment in many developing countries. Since it was also a period of significant transition towards democracy, especially in Latin America, interest has not only centred on the politics of policy reform under crisis conditions, but also on the ability of democratic, as opposed to authoritarian, political systems to cope. This more recent debate has somewhat eclipsed the democracy/development debate and has more usefully focused interest on *policy-making* rather than economic outcomes which are subject to many other, often extraneous, influences.

What, then, are the aspects of democratic regimes which are *thought* to bear on their capacity to initiate and time, appropriate and sustainable economic policies for stabilisation and structural change?

Competitive elections are seen to offer a safety valve for the legal channelling of disaffection and encouraging patience. They provide opportunities for peaceful change and alternative government with popular support and legitimacy to undertake the austerity measures and reforms necessary for adjustment. Where the holding of power alternates, previous experience and further prospects of power promote realism among major opposition groups in economic policy matters and a desire to implement effective policies in order to be re-elected.

There is an expectation of greater consultation with interested and affected groups in policy formulation and more persuasion and less repression, together with the use of partial compensation for losers from policy change. To these expected advantages might be added the fact that a more 'open' and 'free' society will yield access to more ideas and a quicker feedback to government on the way its measures are working.

However, the same democratic rules and conventions can be seen to have corresponding weaknesses in the management of adjustment policies. Elections, or their imminent approach, influence the timing and scope of stabilisation measures: they can swell public expenditure and lead to postponement of unpopular reforms. More fundamentally, democratically elected governments may well become 'populist', giving rise to policies which emphasise growth and short-run distributional goals, and which ignore the risks of inflation and generate excessive deficits.[19]

Under democratic rule, popular groups (trade unions and slum dwellers' associations, etc.) have a greater capacity to disrupt or thwart the implementation of stabilisation policies. Democracies offer more channels than authoritarian rule for protest and more influence on policy-making to subordinate groups; they also create more favourable conditions for the development of strong and independent popular organisations capable of resisting pressure to curtail private consumption. Where workers are free to strike and trade unions are not controlled or suppressed, it is more difficult to curb real wages. Technocrats will normally enjoy more autonomy under authoritarian rulers whereas democratic forces in policy-making will be more fragmented, both within and outside government. The belief that a 'firm hand' is necessary for effective economic adjustment is lacking in a democracy and this may weaken the response and co-operation of civil groups to central appeals, while at the same time weak expectations increase the probability of failure.

The relationship between type of political regime and adjustment policy has been examined empirically in a series of case studies - some of which have studied IMF stabilisation and World Bank structural adjustment experience. These include Remmer (1986, 1990); Sloan and Tedin (1987); Shams (1989); Haggard and Kaufman (1989, 1990); Nelson (1989, 1990), Mosley, Harrigan and Toye (1991).

Empirical evidence

Remmer's (1986) study was based on Latin American experience with IMF stabilisation agreements over the period 1954-84. She concludes that past studies of public policy formation in Latin America have

---

19. A populist model of economic policy (e.g. Allende in Chile 1971-73, Garcia in Peru 1986-88) is expansionist, initially increases real wages, keeps inflation low by price controls, loses foreign exchange reserves, generates shortages and accelerates inflation, capital flight and demonetisation of the economy.

failed to find a strong empirical relation between political regime and policy output or economic performance. Her own study of 114 IMF standby agreements in 9 countries comes to the following conclusions. (a) In respect of 'political will', democratic regimes were not more reluctant to initiate stabilisation programmes. Authoritarian regimes may have inspired greater outside investor confidence but they were no more likely to initiate stabilisation programmes or to survive their political reverberations. (b) There was no statistically significant difference between the performance of authoritarian and democratic regimes in the achievement of policy targets on public expenditure, budget deficit or credit reductions, nor in their willingness to cut real wages and cause unemployment. (c) There was, however, more likelihood of authoritarian systems stabilising inflation in 'polarised' environments than democratic ones. (d) More surprisingly, there was evidence that 'new' democracies were not necessarily more fragile than 'old' democracies in legitimacy and the contingent nature of political support in Latin America; nor was their policy performance in crisis any weaker.

Some work by Haggard and Kaufman (1989) advanced the debate by studying stabilisation experience in developing countries generally. Their perceptions were (a) that authoritarian regimes have not always been better at imposing economic austerity than democracies, and (b) that a distinction between different types of democracy and authoritarian rule is more useful than a simple two-fold distinction. Strong democracies (e.g. Costa Rica), with a tradition of consultation with business and labour, facilitate the acceptance of economic reform (which, it might be added, is a *sine qua non* for the resumption of economic growth). Strong authoritarian governments, characterised by continuity in leadership, insulation from societal pressures and the power to enforce decisions, tend to be relatively successful in imposing the short-term costs of reform (e.g. Korea in the early 1980s) but there may be questions about the sustainability of such reforms. Weak authoritarian governments, especially in Africa, which maintain authority through personalistic patron-client relations, are not so effective at economic policy change; they tend to have more difficulty than strong authoritarian or democratic regimes.

In a later study based on the experience of middle-income countries with inflation and stabilisation, Haggard and Kaufman (1990) conclude that democratic governments are less successful at bringing *high* inflation under control. Also 'transitional' democratic systems seemed, on their evidence, to be less capable of bringing fiscal deficits, public expenditure and credit expansion under control, than continuous democratic or authoritarian systems.

Democratic regimes have more difficulty with stabilisation objectives where party systems or political movements reflect social divisions (e.g. Peru after 1975, Philippines in the early 1970s, and Mexico). Whether political systems are polarised or fragmented seems more pertinent than whether the regime is authoritarian or democratic, since the societal pressures against budget restraint are that much greater. What is more, continued economic stagnation aggravates polarisation and conflict and creates a vicious circle against economic recovery. Constitutional and competitive democratic systems are more likely to sustain macroeconomic stabilisation where there are nationally organised multi-class political parties and movements which mute social conflict, as in Venezuela and, to some extent, Malaysia.

Constitutional democracy does allow changes in regimes through an electoral cycle. These can help new governments in their economic objectives, at least for a honeymoon period. However, democratic regimes have tended to have short-time horizons which makes for less responsible policies. This phenomenon is a function of youthful democracy, but Haggard and Kaufman see some evidence of a political 'learning process' by which parties and politicians extend their time horizons and responsibility as they come to have stronger belief in a longer-term prospect of power via the ballot box.

Further work on 1980s experience by Shams (1989), Nelson (1990), Mosley *et al.* (1991), and Callaghy (1990), drawing on a wide range of studies in developing countries, yields the following important insights on political regime type and specific political institutions in relation to adjustment policy choice.

They confirm that there is no foundation for the belief that authoritarian regimes are more likely to undertake radical economic reform, although some authoritarian dictatorships have embarked on major and sustained reform as well as democratic ones in Africa and elsewhere. It was not a simple issue of democratic versus authoritarian regimes. A more important distinction is between weak and strong executives. Weak governments/central executives - which are unable to command support from divided parties, coalitions, legislatures or key support groups - guarantee delay and paralysis in economic reform and usually result in narrow agendas, as, for example, was the experience of Kaunda in 1983. Where there are strong executives with wide support or a splintered opposition, the initiation of broad programmes of reform is more likely but is not guaranteed. Executives with *strong* support (e.g. Seaga, Garcia, Aquino, Rawlings, Pinochet) -

whether elected or not - were a key to broad if not rapid adjustment initiatives (Nelson, 1990). Shams (1989) similarly argues that, where individual groups in society politically neutralise each other, governments are able to pursue a comparatively independent policy course and effect adjustment successfully.

New centralised military regimes committed to change have some advantages, e.g. Rawlings in 1983. The legitimacy given to new regimes increases their autonomy at least initially, but the emergence of new governments does not ensure sustainable reforms (Mosley *et al.*, 1991).

Nelson (1990) argues that authoritarian regimes are more likely to adopt orthodox reform programmes for stabilisation and structural adjustment, while regimes in transition to democracy adopt non-orthodox programmes and have more difficulty with reform. Established democracies adopt orthodox stabilisation programmes but have difficulty with long-term orthodox structural adjustment policies.

The significance of electoral politics is also explored. Several observers have studied adjustment in the democratic politics of a small country - Jamaica. According to Shams (1989), the distinctive feature of Jamaica's elected governments was their autonomy with regard to any single socio-economic interest group - the private sector, trade unions or the poor - in the formulation of policy. To obtain broad support, politicians are obliged to make compromises when formulating their economic policy platforms. Faced with falling exports and the need to adjust, the Jamaican government in the mid-1980s banked on this relative autonomy and tried to make major policy changes in collaboration with the IMF/World Bank, which were not fully backed by any significant domestic group. Their opposition narrowed Seaga's scope for economic policy change even if it did not threaten it. This resulted in partly inconsistent policy-making and delayed adjustment. Mosley *et al.* (1991) came to the rather agnostic conclusion, that general elections in Jamaica offered an alternative government which could undertake reform even if the 'new broom' did not necessarily sweep clean. However, later on macroeconomic performance and the negotiation of an IMF agreement became an issue in municipal elections. They conclude that in the Jamaican case the regime's general 'willingness to learn' and the desire to avoid the polarisation of the late 1970s were important for democratic electoral politics and effective macroeconomic management.

Nelson (1990), in looking at Jamaica and two other small democracies, Costa Rica and the Dominican Republic, is agnostic about the degree of political consultation and the consensual tactics expected of them. She says (1990:211):

> ... differences between three democracies in consultation and persuasion, political compensation and concern for equality in the course of adjustment suggests caution in generalising about the effects of regime type .... Established democratic institutions make unlikely any strong reliance on simple repression. But in the short run, competitive party systems guarantee neither the inclination nor the skill to use persuasion, engage in consultation or design partial compensation to manage political pressures associated with adjustment.

Whitehead (1990) draws attention to the problems posed for timely macroeconomic management in countries like Mexico which have a fixed presidential term. In Mexico this has generated a political cycle and made it difficult to take tough stabilisation measures in mid-term or in the penultimate year if there was an economic crisis (as in 1982, 1984-5).

In authoritarian regimes, elections or referenda have tended to reduce the autonomy of the state and weaken economic reform efforts, e.g. Zambia in the mid-1980s and Nigeria under Babangida in the late 1980s. In the latter country, a planned transition back to democracy weakened the restructuring impetus, according to Callaghy (1990).

Finally, there has so far been limited systematic assessment of adjustment policies in sub-Saharan African countries under different types of political regimes. Under the auspices of the Overseas Development Institute, Ketley (1991) compared the experience of a small group of semi-democratic countries in sub-Saharan Africa with other, largely authoritarian, regimes during two periods - 1976-81, to reflect the 'pre-adjustment' period and 1982-8, when most countries were forced to make economic adjustments. Quantified indicators of specific economic policies were studied, as well as some measures of economic and social outcomes. Analysis of patterns of revenue mobilisation (direct and indirect taxation and non-tax revenues) and of public expenditure patterns including allocation to health, education, agriculture and defence, showed no statistically significant differences between regime types, though there was an indication that health might have improved more in the more pluralist countries. Nevertheless, the more democratic group of countries (Botswana, The Gambia, Mauritius, Senegal and Zimbabwe) emerged as rather better at the management of public sector budget deficits, while the single-party populist regimes had very high fiscal deficits.

Part III
Summary and Conclusions

From our review of research on the relationship between political regimes and economic policy and performance in the developing world as a whole since the 1950s the following broad points emerge which have relevance for the expectations of those concerned with political and economic prospects for sub-Saharan Africa in the 1990s.

First, there is no systematic evidence that more 'democratic' types of regime - in the sense of being popularly elected, politically competitive and having respect for civil and political rights - are more successful in achieving economic growth or a lower degree of income inequality. At the same time, authoritarian regimes cannot be expected to perform better on these criteria. Some key conditions for economic growth have been the political stability of societies, conditions for the functioning of markets in the allocation of resources, the encouragement and mobilisation of domestic savings and their effective investment, and attention to investment in people's skills. It seems fairly clear that *political instability* in the Third World has been systematically correlated with lower economic growth and lower investment, but it is less clear that this instability is associated with any particular type of political regime, though politically accountable regimes have tended to be more moderate in their response to popular participation and less likely to repress dissent.

The value for wealth creation of policies which rely more on *markets* than state-administered allocation of resources is now more generally accepted than at any time in the last half century. But the relationship between market-oriented policies and political regime type is less clear. There is no assurance from past experience that either democratic or authoritarian political regimes will follow or not follow market-oriented policies. On the other hand, history does suggest that political democracy has been unable to exist unless it is coupled with markets. Markets appear a necessary but not a sufficient condition for sustaining democracy because they provide the basis for stronger independent centres of power to counter that of the state. The chances of well developed, politically accountable systems seem greater at a certain stage of development when an independent business class and intelligentsia have emerged.

It is a myth that the firm hand of authoritarian rule is likely to generate higher domestic *savings* as a basis for growth, whether by 'forcing' public savings or by inegalitarian policies which indirectly assist higher savings rates; especially since past evidence from developing countries suggests that inequality of income does not guarantee higher domestic savings. There is no systematic evidence on whether *investment* rates are higher and investment more productive under more authoritarian regimes. There seems no conclusive evidence that democracies in developing countries have devoted relatively more resources to health and education, while primary expenditures in these sectors have not been assessed. While democracies do not appear to create more equal distribution of income and assets, they do not seem to exacerbate inequality.

It remains ambiguous, in the light of some *historical* reviews, whether societies with more effective checks and balances on central state power from a fairly independent civil society have encouraged faster industrialisation.

The fast-growing economies of Taiwan and Korea seem to owe their success to continuous adjustment of their macroeconomic policies to changing conditions, adherence to a long-term strategy of export-led industrialisation and a purged and reformed bureaucracy. However, no one seems to have established convincingly that their poor civil and political rights record in the past was essential to this.

In economic policy decisions about *adjustment*, especially in response to 'crisis' situations, 1980s experience among developing countries suggests that democratic regimes have no comparative disadvantage in initiating and sustaining difficult policy decisions affecting the economy. They may, however, have faced greater problems in stabilising very high inflation, especially in polarised political/social environments. There must remain considerable scepticism on the importance of regime type in relation to the timing and scope of economic change, especially on a simple dichotomy between democracy and authoritarian rule. 'Strong' democracies with a tradition of consultation could facilitate economic reform but chief executives, even if elected, did not initiate broad economic reform programmes if they were unable to command support from divided parties, coalitions, legislatures or key support groups. While authoritarian regimes were effective in imposing short-term stabilisation measures if they were 'strong' in the sense of having wide support or facing splintered opposition, they were not necessarily effective in sustaining reforms.

Whether a country had an established democracy, a transitional democracy or an authoritarian regime seemed to explain little about the timing and scope of adjustment decisions.

Whatever the regime type, a key factor was the skills of the political leadership, especially in achieving compromise and consensus on policy action. What seems to count in the formulation of policy is not merely the 'rules' of the domestic political game but the ideology of the leadership, the structure of decision-taking, the quality and role played by the bureaucracy, the composition of governing coalitions, the relationship of the government with business and trade unions,and the role of external powers, especially the financial agencies.

Finally, Third World experience so far does not give any assurance that political liberalisation or more representative government will *per se* result in better economic management or more decisive or effective adjustment policies, faster economic growth or less inequality. We return to this issue in the final chapter in considering the prospects for sub-Saharan Africa.

Part IV

Political and Economic Change in Contemporary Sub-Saharan Africa

8
Political Liberalisation and Democratic Transition

Until recently, most observers of African politics were pessimistic about the prospects for democratic rule in the continent. Callaghy (1986:41), for example, argued that 'it would be unwise to predict a widespread flowering of democratic regimes in contemporary Africa. The authoritarian patrimonial state is the norm in Africa and it is likely to remain so.' Similarly, Jackson and Rosberg (1982:82) stated 'we do not expect political history in Black Africa for the foreseeable future to cease providing ample evidence of personal rule', although they acknowledged that there could be a change in leadership orientation over time.

Commentators who equated democracy with Western liberal institutions were sometimes criticised for having a narrow or inappropriate view of the institutional forms that democracy could potentially assume in the African context.[20] There were two sets of objections in this regard. One was that the absence of pre-conditions such as a high level of urbanisation and industrialisation together with universal literacy meant that Western democratic norms were inapplicable, although the examples of multi-party democracies in Botswana, The Gambia and Mauritius appeared to invalidate this thesis. A second line of reasoning, which was often associated with a defence of the

---

20. Linz (1978:5), for example, listed the following criteria: 'Legal freedom to formulate and advocate political alternatives with the concomitant rights to free association, free speech, and other basic freedoms of person; free and nonviolent competition among leaders with periodic validation of their claims to rule; inclusion of all effective political offices in the democratic process; and provision for the participation of all members of the political community, whatever their political preferences. Politically this means the freedom to create political parties and to conduct free and honest elections at regular intervals without excluding any effective political office from direct or indirect electoral accountability.'

one-party state in the 1960s, was that democratic institutions could impede the achievement of national unity and economic development. There were also those who questioned the applicability of Western democratic institutions from the perspective of cultural nationalism, drawing on pre-colonial institutions and traditions as appropriate models for a revitalised African politics (Staniland, 1986).

Such arguments in defence of one-party rule have now come under growing criticism, with democracy increasingly seen as a desirable objective in itself (Ake, 1990; Holmquist, 1989). Moreover, recent political developments draw into question some of the earlier pessimistic assumptions made about the prospects for democratic rule in the continent. Since the late 1980s a significant number of African countries have been undergoing a process of political liberalisation. In some, authoritarian regimes have been edged out by opposition groupings in competitive elections, while in others there has been little more than a verbal commitment to political reform. We begin this chapter by examining what can be learned from the processes of political liberalisation and democratisation in Latin America.

The democratisation process in Latin America

The demise of authoritarian rule in Southern Europe (Greece, Spain and Portugal) in the mid-1970s marked the beginning of a series of democratic transitions in Latin America, South-East Asia, and most recently, Eastern Europe and the former Soviet Union. From the late 1980s, the process of political reform also gathered momentum in sub-Saharan Africa, although it remains unclear to what extent the changes currently under way will find expression in enduring democratic regimes. The experience of democratic transition in Latin America in particular, which is now richly documented in the literature (see, for example, Diamond *et al.*, 1989; O'Donnell *et al.*, 1986), offers insights which can inform our understanding of the political changes currently taking place in Africa.

Authoritarian rule in Latin America was distinct from that which has prevailed in much of Africa for several reasons: 'bureaucratic authoritarianism' was based on strong state institutions controlled by the military and supported by a technocratic elite (businessmen, industrialists, professional economists and planners); it was designed to exclude a politically active civil society; and it was generally inclined towards an open market economy (Cardoso, 1979; Graham, 1980).[21]

In attempting to conceptualise political change in Latin America in the late 1970s and early 1980s, several authors (see, for example, Ethier, 1990b) draw a distinction between the processes of liberalisation and democratisation. Political *liberalisation* is characterised by a series of political reforms which include, *inter alia*, the lifting of emergency measures, the formal recognition of individual and collective rights and, in some cases, the principle of universal suffrage. However, such reforms are introduced in the absence of political compromise between the regime and its opponents, with the result that they are neither guaranteed by the state nor formally accepted by various interest groups, which gives them a provisional and arbitrary character. *Democratisation*, by contrast, refers to the negotiation of a compromise or pact between moderate elements of the regime and opposition forces over the shape and content of political reform. The Latin American experience shows that the terms of the negotiations leading to a compromise varied according to the balance of power between the regime and the opposition in each country. This compromise was usually formulated on the basis of four common elements: (i) an amnesty for offences committed by representatives of the military regime; (ii) the exclusion of radical parties from future governments; (iii) continued repression of armed opposition forces; (iv) the acceptance of a liberal capitalist model of economic development (Ethier, 1990a:11-12).

In this context, the term *democratic transition* is used to refer to an interval between an authoritarian and a democratic regime. There are at least three possible variations of democratic transition: (i) transitions driven largely by external forces; (ii) those resulting from violent intervention by internal forces (revolutions, wars, coup d'états); and (iii) transitions initiated by an internal crisis of the regime. The recent democratic transitions in Southern Europe, Latin America, and increasingly in Africa fall into the third category (O'Donnell *et al.*, 1986). In most countries in Latin America the internal crisis was followed by a phase of *democratic consolidation* marked by the institutionalisation of rules and procedures guaranteeing fundamental

---

21. Callaghy (1986) draws an analogy between the patrimonial state in Africa and the form that it assumed in the early post-colonial period in Latin America, but notes that it differs in many respects from the bureaucratic-authoritarian state.

rights and freedoms, the election of rulers by universal suffrage, party competition and government accountability, all of which presuppose the effective recognition and acceptance of these rules by most interest groups concerned.

Although there are major differences between sub-Saharan African and Latin America, in terms of ethnic composition, economic structure and the form and timing of colonisation, all of which influence contemporary politics, there are similarities in the overall process of democratisation which we are concerned with here.

Pressures for democratic reform in Africa[22]

Contemporary political developments in sub-Saharan Africa are the product of both internal and external pressures, the relative importance of which varies according to the circumstances of individual countries. In what follows, we highlight the main features of the reform process, and examine the way in which different regimes have responded to these pressures.

Domestic pressures

Internal pressures for political reform have been of paramount importance in promoting a process of political liberalisation in Africa, although these have drawn succour from changes taking place elsewhere. In most countries, without opposition movements pressing for constitutional change, authoritarian leaders could continue to ignore outside calls for reform. Moreover, externally-induced political reforms are likely to wither in the absence of an organised internal opposition, or to enable existing regimes to dictate the form and content of political change to their own advantage.

In a marked upsurge in political ferment in the late 1980s, multi-partyism has become the catchword of movements which have sprung up in opposition to authoritarian rule although few have fully elaborated their political programmes. These movements are primarily urban-based and represent a coalition of interests in civil society. Students, trade unionists, intellectuals and professional organisations (principally lawyers and teachers) have been at the forefront of protest movements campaigning for the creation or restoration of multi-party

---

22. The material for this section has been gathered from numerous articles and commentaries in *Africa Confidential*, *African Economic Digest*, *Africa Report*, *West Africa* and *Le Monde* among others.

democracy (Nyong'o, 1987).[23] Young people are also prone to be critical of the record of authoritarian regimes, partly because the rhetoric increasingly justifying one-party rule appears jaded two or three decades after independence, but more importantly because of limited job prospects and restricted mobility (Somerville, 1991). The church, too, has played an important oppositional role in a number of countries in drawing attention to abuses of human rights. The ranks of the opposition have been swelled by dissident politicians and former bureaucrats who have become disenchanted with incumbent authoritarian regimes, especially through their inability to manage the economy, their excessive repression, or their failure to deal effectively with secessionist insurgencies and the prevalence of rampant corruption. While such movements are not entirely new, they have recently gained momentum as a result of the changes taking place in Eastern Europe and South Africa, and the tacit support of donor governments (Carter Center, 1989; 1990).[24]

An ideological shift has also taken place among African intellectuals, many of whom were at one time active proponents of the one-party state, either out of an ideological conviction premised on the pivotal role of the state in effecting social transformation in the post-colonial period, or because they saw the single party as the best defence against ethnic divisions (Ake, 1990). There is now a greater appreciation of the importance of democratic institutions as a means of extending popular participation and legitimacy, even if this has not yet permeated the consciousness of African leaders to any great extent. Few authoritarian rulers retain the support of the intellectuals, who have been subjected to repression over the years because of their willingness to criticise arbitrary and dictatorial rule.

A further critical factor which has increased pressure for more politically accountable and legitimate government has been economic decline and an erosion in living standards. Most African countries experienced a dramatic downturn in their economic fortunes in the 1980s. Recessionary trends in the world economy and climatic

---

23. Development NGOs do not appear to have played much or a role in these movements, although their activities are thought to have contributed to a spread of democratic and participatory values in African societies (Bratton, 1990).

24. The elections held in Namibia in November 1989 provided a fitting culmination to protracted colonial rule and have been an inspiration to those seeking change through the ballot box in other African countries.

uncertainty clearly played a role but economic mismanagement was a decisive factor which prevented governments from devising an effective response to external shocks. Austerity measures introduced under structural adjustment programmes involving public expenditure cutbacks and the removal of subsidies caused economic hardship, especially among the urban poor who have periodically unleashed their discontent in food riots, although the political significance of these has been questioned (Wiseman, 1987; Nelson, 1989).

Popular discontent over economic policies has given vent to movements pressing for political reforms voiced in terms of multi-party democracy in a number of countries, with opposition to structural adjustment providing a powerful impetus, especially since measures adopted thus far have yielded limited tangible benefits. The urban classes, including civil servants, have borne the brunt of public sector cutbacks and retrenchment, at the same time losing out from the abolition of food subsidies and increases in the cost of living. Democracy movements have generally failed to gather much support from the peasantry, many of whom have either benefited more recently from increased producer prices or have been able to insulate themselves by operating in non-official markets.

External influences

It is possible to distinguish three sets of external factors which have contributed to the trend towards political liberalisation in Africa: the revolutions in Eastern Europe, the ending of the Cold War, and aid conditionality.

The spectacular demise of statist regimes in Eastern Europe and the dismantlement of the centralised political system of the Soviet Union have clearly had a demonstration effect in Africa. Authoritarian regimes, especially those wedded to state socialism, have seen the writing on the wall and have accordingly committed themselves to adopting multi-party systems; Mozambique, Angola and most recently, Ethiopia, have all formally abandoned the Marxist-Leninist doctrine and one-party rule.

Political change in Eastern Europe and the former Soviet Union has also been accompanied by a cessation of the Cold War and global realignment. As part of the normalisation of relations between the two superpowers, support for authoritarian regimes of one ideological colouring or another has diminished. The Soviet Union (as it existed) reduced material assistance for its allies in Africa and encouraged them to move in a pluralist direction, while the United States has reconsidered its support for dictatorial pro-Western regimes and insurgency movements in southern Africa. France and Belgium now desist from sending in their troops to prop up discredited dictators, as was the case so often in the past.

The third external factor which has some bearing on political change in Africa is that of the conditions attached by the international financial institutions and bilateral donors to development assistance programmes. Policy-based reforms introduced to promote structural adjustment have encouraged a shift away from statist models of economic management and towards greater decentralisation. More recently, bilateral donors have begun to insist that African governments introduce political reforms, such as a healthier respect for human rights, greater independence for the judiciary, and the removal of press restrictions in order to be eligible for continued aid (Hurd, 1990; Chalker, 1991). Although most donors fall short of demanding a commitment to multi-party democracy, the threat of a termination or a significant reduction in the volume of aid has prompted a number of regimes to seek a popular mandate through competitive elections (ODI, 1992). Indeed, as the Rawlings regime in Ghana recently discovered, a judiciously timed commitment to political reform can bring financial rewards in the form of increased levels of aid.[25]

Regime responses

Democratic transitions in Africa have assumed three principal forms. First, transitions by abandonment of power, where the regime has no control over the process of change and is powerless to influence the end result because of the strength of the opposition. This is followed by the dismantling of authoritarian political institutions and a rapid transfer of power to the opposition. Secondly, transitions by a transfer of power where the regime has limited control over the transition process because of its weakness relative to the opposition, resulting in a compromise on the rules governing the transition process. And thirdly, transitions where the reforms are generated and controlled by the regime because of the absence of significant opposition movements within civil society. The latter takes the form of a controlled process of re-institutionalisation 'from above', in which the regime determines the parameters of political reform in order to ensure some degree of

---

25. The Ghana Government announced that it would introduce multi-party democracy two days before a crucial donor consortium meeting in May 1991 at which pledges from bilateral donors exceeded the volume of assistance initially requested by the government.

continuity. This is likely to result in a more restricted form of democracy.

In the period preceding a democratic transition, authoritarian regimes are no longer able to enforce their authority by coercive means; with a view to their own survival, reformist elements within the regime believe that the political benefits of adopting a more liberal attitude outweigh the costs of repression. This situation arises from a number of developments: the emergence of conflicts or inefficiencies within the repressive apparatus (police, army and intelligence services), the extension of effective controls over repressive forces, and the decline of fear in civil society.

The Carter Center (1991) has identified eight phases of democratic transition in sub-Saharan Africa, beginning with a process of *decay* where the government loses its ability to manage economic and social affairs, manifest in economic decline, chronic inefficiency and social unrest. This leads to more structured forms of political *mobilisation* where calls for fundamental political reform are made by disparate groups opposed to the government. In response to mounting political pressure, political leaders take the *decision* to institute a more legitimate and accountable political system, and concede the principle of competitive elections. In the fourth phase, namely that of *formulation*, details of the transitional programme are worked out, a new draft constitution is drawn up, and a schedule for elections is set. This is followed by *electoral contestation* where political parties and voters are registered, campaigning and voting takes place, resulting in a declaration of the victors. Should the incumbent regime be defeated, there is then a *handover* of power to a democratically elected government. After the new government is sworn in, it undergoes a process of *legitimisation* with the acceptance of the basic tenets of a democratic system. In the final phase of democratic *consolidation* there is widespread respect for fundamental constitutional provisions, especially the rules and procedures governing succession in office. Of course, in practice not all regimes pass through these successive stages, and reversals are possible and the transition process can be extremely protracted.

Authoritarian regimes have responded in differing ways to pressures for political reform. Many have now accepted the principle of multi-party elections but have made limited progress in drawing up a schedule for transition or proposals for constitutional reform. Countries such as Cameroon, Congo, Ghana, and Tanzania fall into this category, where political liberalisation remains tentative. Ruling parties in Senegal and Côte d'Ivoire have actually strengthened their legitimacy by participating in competitive multi-party elections, and, despite accusations of fraud and electoral malpractice, have remained in power. In Gabon, the opposition contested the election result which returned the ruling party to power in September 1990, demanding the dissolution of the assembly and the holding of new elections under international supervision.

In contrast, several regimes have been willing to cede power voluntarily in the face of mass movements pressing for political reform, and to allow competitive elections to take place. Three long-standing authoritarian rulers (of admittedly very small countries) were defeated in elections held in early 1991 and replaced by opposition figures. In February 1991, President Aristides Pereira of Cape Verde was voted out of office in free and competitive multi-party elections. His defeat was followed in quick succession by those of Mathieu Kérékou in Benin and Pinto da Costa in São Tomé and Príncipe the following month. Kérékou's defeat at the polls was especially significant in view of his tenacity in the face of previous threats to his regime over the past 18 years, underpinned by his willingness to use force to suppress dissent. Most dramatically of all, Kenneth Kaunda of Zambia experienced a humiliating defeat in elections held in October 1991, handing over power to Frederick Chiluba's Movement for Multi-party Democracy (MMD). In these countries, democratic transition has taken place through a process typified by a transfer of power where the regime is weak relative to the forces of the opposition.

Other regimes have sought to control the form and pace of political reform with minimal consultation in order to produce a favourable outcome which would not threaten their power base. For example, the Guinean President, Lansana Conte, introduced a very gradual transitional programme before opposition to his military regime intensified to a point where there would be few other options. The Babangida regime in Nigeria has also sensed which way the wind is blowing and has committed itself to a programme of selective democratisation from above. Only two parties have been officially recognised for the 1992 elections, one left of centre and the other right of centre (Oyediran and Agbaje, 1991). In the Nigerian context such a move places an unduly narrow straitjacket on political activity, but allows the regime to assume the mantle of democratic legitimacy in the eyes of the international community.

The national conference has come to play a key role in facilitating the process of democratic transition in countries such as Niger, Zaire and Togo, although in the latter, it did not prevent the military from ousting the transitional government. In some cases political incumbents have sought to manipulate the outcome of such conferences by ensuring that their supporters predominate numerically. The pace of political liberalisation is critically determined by the powers of sovereignty assumed by the conference. Where ruling incumbents have successfully resisted the delegation of sovereignty the process of reform has become more attenuated and the likelihood of change less certain. But when conference delegates have successfully assumed powers of sovereignty, as in Togo and Niger, regime incumbents have been publicly disgraced and their misdeeds exposed for all to see. Another tactic, exemplified by President Mobutu of Zaire, is to encourage the formation of a multiplicity of political parties and the co-option of key opposition leaders into ministerial positions in order to fragment the opposition and dissipate any organised threat to the incumbents' continued rule. This type of protracted transition would appear to be the dominant form in Africa, where reforms are introduced over a period of time during which authoritarian rulers try at all costs to avoid losing power.

In other countries, authoritarian leaders have resorted to violence in order to curb strikes and mass protests, with the military intervening to preserve order. Yet unlike previous episodes in African politics, the new leaders of Mali and Ethiopia have accepted the need for democratic reforms, even if they are dragging their feet over introducing constitutional amendments to legalise political parties and in announcing an election date. Dictatorial regimes in Chad, Somalia and Liberia have been violently overthrown in the aftermath of civil war; although the victors in Chad and Somalia have nominally committed themselves to holding elections, there seems little immediate prospect of this happening until some measure of political stability is achieved. In the absence of a central authority which commands widespread popular support, secessionist pressures have strengthened and ethnic rivalries have deepened.

Finally, several countries continue to adhere to the single-party model despite pressures for political reform. In sharp contrast with the democratic upsurge in other countries, Mugabe's regime in Zimbabwe was intent on legalising a one-party state but backed down following opposition from within the ruling party. The pragmatists sensed that the negative repercussions of such a move, particularly among the international donor community, would outweigh the ideological benefits of one-party rule and successfully resisted Mugabe's initiative. Daniel Arap Moi of Kenya had strongly resisted any change in the one-party system despite mounting donor pressure, and vigorously suppressed political dissent or any attempts by the opposition to campaign for free and fair elections, but he too finally succumbed in December 1991 to calls for political reform by accepting the case for multi-party democracy.

A number of African regimes, among them Zimbabwe and Senegal, fall within the category of semi-democratic, a term which is used to refer to countries in which the effective power of elected officials is limited, there are restrictions on political parties, and the fairness of elections is open to question, such that electoral outcomes deviate from popular preferences, or where civil and political liberties are subject to limitations (Coulon, 1988).

All this suggests that there is likely to be considerable variation in the types of regime that emerge from this process of political reform and transition. A score-card of the number of regimes which have progressed towards multi-party democracy does not shed much light on the nature of intermediary forms of political participation which are expressed through greater competition within a single party or increased scope for consultation and accountability, and which also fall within the ambit of increased democratisation. Tanzania has always claimed that it provides for a level of open debate within the single party and that participation is encouraged through mass organisations affiliated to the party. Kenya allowed voters to choose between competing candidates even if they did not represent opposition parties. The point to note here is not that restricted forms of democracy are necessarily a desirable outcome but that there is a possibility that the one-party system will continue to remain the norm in a number of African countries, albeit in a more liberal guise or with populist overtones. This warrants a consideration of the potential for increased inner-party democracy. It is possible that a single-party system with scope for open debate and representation of minority interests may actually be more democratic than a multi-party system where there is minimal public consultation and accountability; a comparison between Nyerere's Tanzania and the civilian government of President Shagari in Nigeria is instructive in this regard. For these reasons, it is likely that several regimes currently undergoing a process of political liberalisation will also end up as 'semi-democracies' (Diamond *et al.*, 1990).

Although political liberalisation is now well under way in a number of African countries, there is considerable uncertainty over its future direction and likely impact, both on the underlying structure of politics and on economic policy management. Some observers express doubt about the true extent and the likely beneficiaries of political reform. In this respect, Anyang' Nyong'o (1988:74) argues that, in the absence of a political culture of participation and accountability, multi-party democracy is likely to remain confined to competition among the political elite to the exclusion of the masses. Enfranchisement does not necessarily lead to empowerment, since universal suffrage does not guarantee access to political decision-making. Other commentators treat contemporary manifestations of political liberalisation as cosmetic reforms designed to please outsiders, or to ensure the continued dominance of authoritarian leaders in the face of popular discontent (Ellis, 1991).

A final consideration is whether the current wave of political reforms represents anything distinctively new and whether any historical precedents exist in the post-colonial period which offer insights into contemporary developments. Many commentators believe that African politics has come full circle, from democratic political forms at independence towards authoritarianism and military rule in the late 1960s and 1970s, with signs of a return to democracy from the late 1980s. It is difficult to point to a comparable period in recent African political history when the democratic impetus was as pronounced as it is today. Although there were democratic interludes when military regimes ceded power to civilian governments in the 1970s, as in Nigeria and Ghana, these were generally short-lived and did not reflect a lasting or widespread trend. While the democratic political changes currently under way in a growing number of African countries do not represent a totally new phenomenon, the defeat of four incumbent regimes through competitive multi-party elections in the space of one year was certainly without precedent.

A more thorny question concerns the sustainability of the current reforms. Are more countries likely to follow the route to multi-party democracy, and what is the likelihood that democratic regimes which have come to power in recent months will endure? The more enthusiastic proponents of political reform in Africa are convinced that a democratic revolution is sweeping the continent and that democracy is here to stay (Carter Center, 1990). Other observers err on the side of caution. With recourse to the historical experience of Western democracies, they argue that democratic transition is a painful and protracted process which cannot be compressed into a few short years or imposed by outsiders (Dunn, 1986). In the next chapter we explore some of these themes in rather more detail and speculate on some of the possible tensions that may emerge between the impetus for greater political accountability on the one hand and for improved economic policy management on the other.

9
Prospects for Sustained Political Reform and Improved Economic Management

In the previous chapter we saw that a process of political liberalisation and incipient democratisation was now under way in a number of sub-Saharan African countries. This appears to draw into question earlier pessimistic assumptions about the prospects for democracy in the continent. Nevertheless, there is considerable variation in views over the likely extent of political liberalisation and its potential to be sustained over the longer term.

In addition to the more general lessons that emerge from our review of the literature on the politics of economic policy-making, there are several more specific issues which relate to the African experience. The first concerns the relationship between political reform and factors such as ethnicity, clientelism and the functioning of legislatures. The second is about the implications of economic reform for governance, and focuses on potential tension between pressures for more open and accountable government on the one hand and more efficient decision-making and improved economic performance on the other, since compatibility between these two objectives is by no means assured.

Before we move on to consider these issues, it may be useful to hark back to those factors considered in Chapters 1 and 4 which help to explain the persistence of democratic politics in countries such as Botswana and Mauritius in view of the prevalence of authoritarian rule in sub-Saharan Africa for most of the post-independence period. Do these countries have distinctive features which are not found in other African countries or do they offer lessons which have a wider application?

Democratic precedents in Africa

Both Botswana and Mauritius are former British colonies. In Botswana there is a similarity of language and cultural traditions in which no single ethnic group has dominated politics. Extensive consultation with traditional communal assemblies has widened political participation even though there is minimal independent interest group activity. In Mauritius there is a common spoken language and official tolerance for minority languages, and broad consensus over the desirability of multi-party democracy. Ethnically-based politics persist in an island where 70 per cent of the population are of Indian origin, but caste, religious and urban-rural cleavages cut across racial affiliations. Political leaders are subject to intense public scrutiny, radical political activity has remained within assumed constitutional and legal norms, and there is widespread agreement over the merits of a mixed economy.

A related consideration is the political culture of individual countries. Some countries in Africa have long traditions of democratic decision-making, which in part derive from pre-colonial customary norms. In Botswana, for example, it has been argued that the traditional tribal councils play an important role in channelling local concerns to national leaders and holding the same leaders accountable for their decisions (Molutsi and Holm, 1990). However, at the same time there are limits on the scope for opposition activity and the same party has been in power since independence.

Another factor which shaped the political culture of a number of African countries was the introduction of partial democratic rule in the period prior to independence. For example, Diamond (1988) claims that the experience of legislative participation helped to inculcate a democratic ethos in countries such as Ghana and Senegal at an early stage of their political development.

It remains unclear to what extent these countries provide valid lessons which are of significance elsewhere since in many ways they are rather special cases. On the one hand, Botswana and Mauritius are small in terms of population compared to other countries in Africa, and the latter has high educational levels by African standards. Since it is located some 1,500 miles off the east African coast, Mauritius has relatively weak links with mainland Africa. On the other hand, the experience of these two countries indicates that consultation and openness are important features of political life and create a more conducive climate for the sharing of ideas and debating of policy options. The case of Mauritius, in particular, suggests that political accommodation is possible in ethnically fragmented societies, perhaps because there are multiple cleavages and not simply sharply opposed ethnic groupings sharing a similar language, customs and values.

The sustainability of political reform

Our interest here concerns the potential sustainability of democratic transition, with respect to ethnicity and the accommodation of interest-group pressures within a political framework dominated by patronage.

Ethnicity

Many observers are cautious about the prospects for lasting political change in view of the destabilising potential of ethnic and cultural rivalries. After independence the creation of one-party states was often justified on the grounds of maintaining national unity in the face of what were seen as divisive regional and ethnic loyalties (see Chapter 1). Yet, far from being excluded, influential leaders from minority ethnic groups were accommodated into state structures by means of patronage and employment. Political rivalry in one-party authoritarian states generally revolved around a struggle for a share of public resources, which was often ethnically based. Occasionally, when state resources were monopolised by a politically dominant ethnic group, resentment erupted in an orgy of violence as, for example, in Burundi in 1972. Regional discontent in some cases gave birth to secessionist movements (as in Ethiopia, Nigeria and Zaire), but none were successful in pressing their claims to independent statehood.

The spectre of ethnic conflict is still invoked by entrenched adherents of one-party rule (until recently by President Moi in Kenya) to justify their rejection of multi-party democracy. This concern, however, is not altogether unfounded. It is all the more compelling in countries where several large ethnic groups predominate and compete for power. Political aspirants anxious to secure a share of state resources have been willing to play the ethnic card in their pursuit of office. New opposition parties in many countries have an identifiable, though not always explicit, ethnic base. Political incumbents have also proved adept at manipulating ethnic and regional loyalties in a cynical attempt to remain in power. On the other hand, as the process of democratisation has taken root, several regimes have introduced safeguards to prevent a resurfacing of such tensions.

Nigeria's current experiment in controlled democratisation from above is primarily an exercise aimed at controlling ethnic and regional rivalries which have been the cause of so much political upheaval since independence. Special constitutional provisions were introduced by the country's military rulers with the return to civilian rule in 1979 to ensure representation of various ethno-regional interests. There was an implicit attempt to build ethnic coalitions by including major ethnic interests in the decision-making apparatus through weighted federal appointments to ministerial posts and parastatals. The principle of ethnic accommodation was carried into the structures of the governing party which ensured that it drew support from different ethnic regional groups. While this approach to creating a more 'inclusive' politics boosted the popularity of the ruling party, it may also have been partly responsible for fuelling clientelism by increasing the number of claimants on public resources.[26]

On a more optimistic note, the experience of Botswana and Mauritius suggests that ethnic and linguistic differences are not in themselves inimical to multi-party democracy, but that much depends on the mechanisms employed to channel and mediate these cleavages. In Mauritius the adoption of a 'best-loser' system guarantees ethnic minority representation in parliament, using the principle of proportionality. Although most members are elected on a simple plurality system in single-member constituencies, there is legal provision for the eight most successful losing candidates to be selected from ethnic communities deemed to be under-represented in the parliament. This provision makes it possible for political coalitions to be formed which include representatives of various communities (Rothchild and Foley, 1988:239).

Another mechanism employed in some states to accommodate ethnic and sub-national pressures has been that of regional autonomy. In Nigeria the federal system represents one attempt in this direction, with the creation of new states in response to demands from newly-politicised regional and ethnic constituencies. Political liberalisation has meant that regimes in countries which have experienced continuous internal upheaval are less likely to use force to repress secessionist pressures. Some are now exploring the possibility of granting greater autonomy to minority ethnic groups (for example, the Tuaregs in Mali) in order to allay the threat of secession. Others, such as the new revolutionary government in Ethiopia, are prepared to concede independence (to Eritrea), although this would seem to be an exceptional case, reflecting the particular complexion of the coalition forces which ousted the Mengistu regime.

---

26. Rothchild and Foley (1988:241) see this as an inevitable part of the political *quid pro quo* of ethnic accommodation: 'If the politics of inclusiveness sometimes gives rise to political payoffs and backscratching within the dominant political elite, thereby complicating the process of increasing aggregate productiveness, it nonetheless has the positive effect of promoting interethnic cooperation.'

Under authoritarian rule ethnic interests were incorporated into political structures through informal power-sharing arrangements, whereas more formalised constitutional provisions may well become increasingly necessary in order to promote stability and genuine political accountability as political liberalisation takes hold. The new democratic regimes in Africa may employ 'consociational' mechanisms along the lines of those introduced in Mauritius and Nigeria to accommodate changing patterns of patron-client relations but this will depend in the final analysis on the skill and aptitude of the political leadership.

Despite such provisions, it remains likely that ethnic and regional identities, which are deeply embedded in the social structure of many African countries (but are not always the source of conflict), will remain a potent source of political instability for many years to come, given the proclivity of political leaders in the past to manipulate such identities to their own advantage. This points to the importance of political culture in cultivating a healthy respect for institutional rules and procedures for governing democratic political activity, and constitutional provisions to prevent any single ethnic or cultural group from dominating politics. It is also possible that the growing political assertiveness of 'modern' interest groups such as trade unions and business associations may cut across ethnic and regional ties and create the basis for new types of political expression and reduce the importance of ethnic coalition-building.

Civil society

It is often argued that the existence of a vibrant civil society is essential to the growth and persistence of democratic politics and provides by definition a countervailing force to that of the state. Strong and representative interest groups can foster political awareness and participation. They are also important instruments of democratic socialisation and renewal.

As discussed in Chapter 5, civil society in Africa contains a wide variety of groups and individuals who share the common position of being outside the state. These range from traditional community bodies to ethnic associations and class-based organisations such as trade unions and farmers' associations. Although these groups have not been engaged in active conflict with the state, they have not been simply dormant and, there is, of course, considerable variation between individual countries. Many groups have consequently opted for a strategy of disengagement from state structures, although there are signs of greater assertiveness and vitality in the present climate of political liberalisation.

There are several promising possibilities in this regard, although these need to be approached with some caution. First, any retreat of the state and contraction of the bureaucracy will widen the space for associational activity, creating new opportunities for political involvement by previously excluded groups. This has found expression in some countries in broad-based democracy movements which bring together a wide range of organisations and associations into opposition coalitions (see Chapter 8). There may also be scope for a greater interchange of ideas with the retreat of a 'statist' ideology and increased freedom of expression and association which could form the basis for the emergence of a more pluralist political culture. Party-building is clearly central to this process, although this would have to come about through the reinvigoration of moribund single parties at the grassroots or the formation of parties which draw on new constituencies, perhaps corresponding to class-based rather than ethnically-grounded interest groups, and increased scope for parliamentary activity.

Second, the policy environment is also changing, with increased scope for consultation in the formation of public policy, which may bring new groups into the bargaining process. This could stimulate the involvement of business associations, which have not generally played a prominent role in influencing policy formation. Many groups in civil society, especially peasants, have retreated from state organisations and regulations into the informal economy. These could return to a more active political role if subsistence agriculture, smuggling and migration become more difficult and costly while deregulation provides greater economic incentives. 'Voice' could therefore become a more promising option than 'exit' (Herbst, 1990a).

A further consideration is whether a 'corporatist' model would be appropriate for African conditions, at a time of economic crisis, weakened state authority and desire for political change (Nyang'oro and Shaw, 1989). The essential idea is for selected organised interest groups - probably umbrella organisations (such as business organisations, trade unions) - to participate actively in policy-making, rather than just merely lobbying the government. The policy-making process is thus internalised. Underlying this approach is the concept of a 'political exchange' in which these privileged interest groups negotiate with the state, and among themselves, in order to arrive at a consensus on policy action. The *quid pro quo* for the state is some guarantee of compliance with the chosen policy by the organisations, including possibly some 'self-regulatory' functions. The advantage claimed for such a model is the establishment of arrangements for reconciling divergent interests and conflicts in policy-making which reduces the burden on the state bureaucracy. A more systematic process of consultation than purely *ad hoc* lobbying might emerge, though this presupposes a considerable professional and analytical capacity in these organisations as well as a power to deliver the agreement and the compliance of their often diverse membership. Nevertheless, the upshot might be a more consistent and workable set of policies.

Given the exclusive nature of this corporatist model there must be doubts about its appropriateness in contemporary African societies where the weaker interests in society have been so neglected in the past. It runs the high risk of actually strengthening the power of the interests which are best organised and funded. It hardly seems a promising option in countries where producer associations have usually been formed through coercion or have been taken over and their leaders co-opted by the state. Nor does it seem very feasible in countries which are mainly agricultural and where a large informal economy exists. It is certainly not an obvious substitute for representative political democracy in Africa and does not seem to complement current moves towards political openness.

Finally, in their general encouragement of African regimes towards 'open' government and greater 'responsiveness' to their citizens, aid donors have been rather vague in specifying the forms this should take, even though they apparently think it is appropriate and consistent with economic policies which encourage wealth creation (ODI, 1992). The most basic proposition is that governments might be expected to consult those interest groups which have some legitimacy through the size of their membership, as well as their advocacy of well-formulated positions on policy issues which represent a consensus among their members. These might be sectoral organisations of producers or umbrella organisations such as Chambers of Commerce or Manufacturing, but they might also be trade unions, professional associations or community organisations. Consultation and openness to lobbying by such groups in a formal and public way provides a countervailing influence to the state, and should also help to bring about more effective and pragmatic policy formulation. Regimes stand to gain greater political legitimacy if they are willing to take account of the concerns of a wide range of interests when deciding their action, provided the policy output is credible and can be seen to represent a fair compromise with these interests.

Nevertheless, some important questions remain about such a process in Africa. Many of these interests will be in conflict, and the already strained administrations of African countries will not find conflict management of this kind easy, especially when the articulation of such positions is formally and publicly encouraged. It is not obvious that all important interests will have an effective voice; the more powerful and well-resourced ones are bound to have an advantage. This suggests that any encouragement of formal representation should be accompanied by positive efforts to assist the weaker and less vocal sections of the population with funds and professional capability. Since few states have a good record in encouraging comments and criticism of their actions, there may be a role for donors to assist in this type of development. Good examples would be the strengthening of organisations representing small manufacturing and trading businesses and small farmers' associations, to help ensure that regulatory policies and public services and their implementation are not biased against such groups but rather to assist them in their economic activities.

Legislative assemblies

Elected legislative assemblies have the special capacity to influence and review decision-making at the national level while preserving the basis for a pluralistic political system. Such assemblies exist in a number of African countries although they have had little effective power or autonomy under authoritarian rule (see Chapter 4). In the debate on multi-partyism in Africa, there has been surprisingly little discussion of the prospects for transforming them from 'councils of convenience' (usually instruments of state elites to legitimise their professed democratic credentials) into 'councils of consent' which would articulate and respond to the interests of their constituents as a matter of course.

Sissons and Snowiss (1979) spell out the conditions which are favourable or unfavourable for the revival of effective legislatures. In their view it is not enough for the assembly to be representative; it must also be grounded in the capacity to influence law-making. Elections have vigour only if the legislature has sufficient autonomy to influence public policy. First, there needs to be an ideology of legitimacy for legislatures to have such an influential role which is easier to achieve when the ruling elites embrace some variant of representative democracy. Second, there needs to be a specific, perhaps new, social class or coalition, which finds a legislature a useful instrument for its own interests. Third, an effective role for the assembly is more likely where the organisation of the executive is based on decentralised authority and there is a tradition of local political autonomy. Fourth, since elected assemblies encourage the expression of divisive and conflicting interests there needs to be a strong willingness in deeply divided societies to seek consensus (as in Mauritius), to avoid electoral retaliation and to resolve social conflict through peaceful political competition. Finally, the more ethnically polarised the society the greater the challenge to a revived and effective legislature, although, as we have argued, this factor is not necessarily an impediment to political and institutional change (Lonsdale, 1981; Diamond, 1988).

In the light of these quite demanding conditions it is not surprising that, for sub-Saharan Africa, it is difficult to take a sanguine view of prospects for the revival of elected national assemblies to provide the basis for increased legitimacy, to check the excesses of executive power, to debate policies and to create laws. When the stakes are so high for executive power-holding, it is difficult to see why elites should redistribute effective political power to representative legislators. However, there are economic and financial pressures on African rulers, and significant changes in economic strategy - to some extent forced on them - may in turn induce political change.

Patronage, clientelism and economic policy reform

Of particular interest is what may happen to patronage and clientelism under political liberalisation and economic policy reform. There are at least four possible outcomes. In the *status quo* scenario little change will take place in basic configurations of the patronage system. According to this line of reasoning, changes in the form of regime (i.e. from authoritarian to more democratic types) would leave the underlying structure intact, since by its very nature the patrimonial state will change only slowly and incrementally (Callaghy, 1986).

A second possibility is that the whole system will collapse, with a replacement of clientelism by 'modern' competitive politics, although this seems rather unlikely, since in most African countries the business class and the trade unions are relatively weak.

The third possible scenario is where the sweeping aside of clientelist politics leaves a void. Hawthorn (1991), for example, argues that the process of economic reform could give rulers the chance to remove powerful members of the state elite who had hitherto relied on patronage, and replace them with a new breed of technocrats. Interestingly he sees this development as running counter to the impetus towards greater political competition, since it undermines patron-client networks but puts nothing in their place. It may also undermine the formation of factions which arguably constitute the basis for a reinvigorated competitive politics in Africa in the long term.

A fourth scenario, which in our view is the most probable, is where patronage remains, but as an integral feature of a more 'inclusive' politics. The experience of democratic rule in Nigeria between 1979 and 1983 would appear to bear out this possibility, since elite competition over the control of state resources and state offices intensified during this period, resulting in increased levels of corruption within the patrimonial state (Joseph, 1983). Similarly in Ghana, during the period 1969-72, participation in competitive elections resulted in the enrichment of big patrons, which was politically destabilising (Chazan, 1988). This is also likely to be the case in some of the newly-emerging democracies elsewhere in the continent, where interest groups excluded from the political process in the past are actively seeking to benefit from the fruits of office. At the same time, those who previously benefited from their proximity to the state, either through holding office or employment or the granting of special favours, stand to lose from democratisation and are unlikely to cede power and influence voluntarily. The form and extent of patronage politics will be strongly influenced by the effects of economic policy reforms on the size and availability of public resources.

There are at least three ways in which economic reform programmes may impact on the political behaviour of ruling elites in sub-Saharan Africa (Nelson, 1989). First, the regime loses support from certain key groups in civil society (public sector employees and the urban poor) who do not benefit, at least in the short run, from the policy changes and will often lose out altogether. Others can gain, especially peasant producers, from pricing and marketing reforms. The implication is that the regime will be looking to switch constituencies in search of continued support and legitimacy. Second, the economic changes are likely to undermine the resources and scope for patronage via reduced state control over the allocation of public expenditure, credit, and foreign exchange and the power to introduce subsidies. Third, regimes which have traditionally mobilised support through patron-client relationships rather than votes will feel more insecure politically.

How will incumbent regimes respond? Alternative scenarios have been painted. Perhaps the most optimistic is that of Abernethy (1989) and Lancaster (1989). Authoritarian rulers may conclude that it is in their own interest to broaden political participation to include the rural food-producing beneficiaries of reform, as a significant supportive constituency. There is also an increased awareness of the potential and tenacity of popular opposition which can no longer be simply repressed through the use of force. Thus structural adjustment may be a precursor to greater electoral democracy. There are already signs of this, although it is too soon to assess the thoroughness of moves towards greater political freedom and multi-party elections.

Herbst (1990b), in perhaps the most systematic exploration of possible scenarios, suggests that the decline in the power of patronage might induce African political leaders to reinvigorate their parties at the grassroots - a course which they had neglected to take since independence because patronage offered them an easier option. The economic decentralisation implicit in moves towards market systems of allocation is also likely to increase pressures on governments to decentralise their political structures. However, experience in Asia suggests that market-oriented economic policies are able to co-exist with authoritarian governments for a long time before they give rise to irresistible pressures for democratisation (Wade, 1991). Another possible response to these pressures is greater coercion on the part of some rulers as they become more insecure. They possess fewer means for buying off restive factions in the face of tensions generated by minority ethnic groups who may well become more vocal politically as a result of structural adjustment policies.

In several African countries opposition leaders who have come to power as a result of competitive elections (such as Nicephore Soglo, the president of Benin) have a strongly technocratic orientation, with experience of working as senior-level professionals in the World Bank, the IMF and the UN specialised agencies.[27] The political leadership in countries undergoing democratic transition (for example, the Chiluba government in Zambia) has generally been committed to economic policy reform where this has been initiated, but the extent to which it is willing to introduce mechanisms to ensure greater accountability and transparency remains unclear. It is quite possible that, in their desire to improve economic policy-making and, by

---

27. This phenomenon is not restricted to the emergent democracies. Governments in countries such as Cameroon, Congo, Gabon and the Ivory Coast, where the process of political liberalisation is less certain, have also appointed officials with experience of working in multilateral agencies to senior positions in the administration as a means of reversing the legacy of economic mismanagement.

implication, economic performance, there will be little compulsion on the part of proponents of economic policy reform to encourage consultation and to widen access to the decision-making process.

Indeed, technocratic regimes may be forced to retain elements of the patronage system in the interests of preserving political stability. Such changes could run counter to the imperatives of bureaucratic efficiency in slowing down the pace of reform and placing obstacles in the way of reform measures, especially those that threaten the livelihoods of important interest groups such as trade unions and public sector employees. In such a situation, patronage will in all probability persist, but in a different form. Formal 'consociational' mechanisms will determine access to public resources and positions of influence, which will continue to be dominated by elite interests, even if they differ in their ethnic and regional composition.

Lessons from history

It may be instructive at this point to consider historical parallels which may give some long- term perspective to the prospects for democracy, the decline of the patrimonial state and the emergence of modern capitalism in Africa. Callaghy in two separate essays (1988, 1986) reviews experience (a) from early modern Europe and (b) from post-colonial Latin America since the early nineteenth century. Drawing on European historical experience, Callaghy (1988) argues that there is a strong parallel between the modern African state and the early modern European mercantilist state. Indeed, in his view, it was this historical model which was imposed by the colonial powers in Africa. The state in early modern Europe had an overriding political but not economic logic; it pursued mercantilist policies to increase its strength both internally and externally. Historical examples of patrimonial capitalism abound where the state became the easiest source of wealth and access to power, although these were hardly conducive to the development of modern capitalism. With European mercantilism the political 'retarding factor' was the arbitrariness of patrimonial rule, which reduced the certainty and calculability vital to modern capitalism. The transition was only accomplished when political dominance gave way to economic logic; political arbitrariness was contained through the gradual creation of a legal and administrative apparatus, so reducing the risks for productive capitalist accumulation and market transactions.

History suggests that we should not exaggerate either the pace or the permanence with which a more favourable economic and political environment is achieved. Rather, this shift occurred slowly and unevenly as rising bourgeois elements ceased to demand special protection and favours and began to expect to make predictable calculations without having to 'pay' for them each time via patron-client ties. This allowed the emergence of capitalism in a context facilitated by market exchange, private ownership, markets for factors of production, and a rational monetary system.

A historical lesson which Hyden (1983) has drawn is that there will be no significant discipline on the state until a more robust autonomous capitalist class emerges in Africa. This may take a long time as it did historically in Europe, and there is no guarantee that it will act as the political midwife for democracy, especially since most African countries, with a few exceptions (Kenya, Nigeria and Côte d'Ivoire), possess small bourgeoisies which play a relatively minor role in national politics (Dunn, 1986). However, Sandbrook (1985), for example, has drawn attention to a 'short-cut' approach in the evolution of state capitalism in Germany, Japan and Taiwan, which may yet find its application in Africa.

A comparison of contemporary Africa with the evolution of post-colonial Latin American economies since the early nineteenth century is also illuminating since they share certain common features, with similar primary producing economies dependent on a narrow range of exports, and centralised authoritarian states. Callaghy (1986) makes a careful comparison but draws unpromising parallels, since Latin American political history was unstable. Most countries had a predominantly authoritarian patrimonial state for long periods, interspersed with pseudo- and quasi-democratic forms of politics up to the 1890s. The nature of this patrimonial administrative state changed only slowly and incrementally. There were exceptions; Costa Rica and Colombia were democratic from an early period. Although Chile developed representative institutions from the 1830s (elected Presidents with constitutionally designated successors), parliamentary accountability developed slowly (Diamond *et al.*, 1989). From this Callaghy (1986:50) concludes rather pessimistically that 'it is unlikely though not impossible to have a long-lasting democracy in an early patrimonial administrative state. The combination of political skill and fortuitous circumstances required is rare.'

Only time will reveal whether these views hold true in the African context. In general, economic reform in Africa has preceded any significant political reform, though the sustainability of economic reforms remains in doubt, even in those countries which have initiated them. There is clearly a need for more research on the interaction between the two processes, especially in countries where these are proceeding simultaneously, and to separate out the different factors at work prompting political and economic reform. More importantly, as political liberalisation takes hold, it raises the question of how patronage will be reconciled with effective economic management in the new democratic polities in Africa. This forms the subject of the final part of this chapter.

Will political liberalisation improve economic management?

There is a current view that more open, politically accountable government will mean more effective economic management (ODI, 1992). The process of political change is at an early stage in Africa. Hence, we can only speculate on how such changes might affect economic decision-making.

We define a process of political *liberalisation* as one in which the fear of repression is relaxed and there are constitutional guarantees of a range of political freedoms (especially the recognition of the right of opposition groupings to function and to express dissent); in which there is greater independence for legislative assemblies where they still exist, and freedom of the press.

A process of increased political *accountability* we see as a move towards more inclusive politics, even within a single-party system, through the introduction of measures to extend societal participation in political decision-making. This implies the setting up of mechanisms of consultation (formal and informal) between the state, political parties and principal interest groups and procedures under which the state airs its policies in advance of their implementation. Finally political accountability means that state actions and policy decisions are transparent and open to greater public scrutiny and comment in order to discourage rent-seeking activities and clientelism.

A process of *democratisation* involves the introduction of universal suffrage and genuine political competition with free and fair elections to decide who will take power.

Likely areas of compatibility

The main question that concerns us here is whether political change of this kind would result in better economic management than we have witnessed in sub-Saharan Africa over the past 25 years.

There are several ways in which political liberalisation may do so via more public airing of alternative economic policy options, criticism of the working of existing policies and publicly articulated expression from a wider range of previously excluded interests on how the policies affect them. This could come from a legalised political opposition, revived assemblies, greater public debate and a stronger voice from existing and previously excluded independent interest groups, all of which should encourage a wider agenda of policy issues. It will particularly be so if policy questions can become important issues in both intra-party and inter-party politics and if they can become central to parliamentary and public debate. Legislative assemblies have been bypassed or neutered as fora for independent scrutiny of state actions, debate of proposed policies and approval of government legislation and expenditure. With greater freedom and authority, these institutions could potentially become an informed source of critical and constructive examination of public expenditure and public sector management.

First, if state elites come to feel more 'secure' in office because they seek, and are seen, to represent a wider range of interests, they can potentially derive further legitimacy by a willingness to consider a broader range of policy options, instead of the rather narrow economic agendas that typified authoritarian governments which changed only under crisis conditions and in response to external pressures.

Second, with wider political responsiveness there should be greater willingness to change inappropriate policies. Previously, state elites often appeared to have been frozen into inappropriate patterns of policy for fear of disturbing their narrow client base and the balance of their supportive coalitions. The more societal interests that are included in the political frame, the greater flexibility there should be to make changes of policy which may hurt some but will also benefit others. Past failure of policy to anticipate and adjust to changing conditions until a crisis situation was reached, might give way to more flexible and adaptive policy in a freer, more open and inclusive type of politics. Response to wider interests might well have generated a more effective policy configuration than occurred in many African states - preventing over-regulation, poor marketing and prices, and improving inadequate public services to those politically neglected groups which followed a strategy of 'exit' rather than 'voice' in the past (Hirschman, 1981).

Third, policy has largely been made in small closed circles in Africa with very little or no consultation with affected, or other, interests. A more participatory politics with greater and wider consultation *before* the policy is finally promulgated should improve its credibility and effectiveness. Similarly regular monitoring and feedback on how existing policy is implemented and is working, should improve the chances of modification or reversal where necessary. Independent economic interests such as business associations, or groups of small farmers, which cross ethnic or regional divisions, do not seem to have had the capacity or influence in Africa to articulate their perspectives on public policies and the way they work. The business community appears to have worked mainly through informal channels, and more on the implementation of policy than on its formulation - seeking exceptions, evasions and special privileges mainly in the areas of taxation, trade, credit and foreign exchange and some investment policies. This way of proceeding has to some extent reflected the tradition of patronage in Africa.

Fourth, political liberalisation should encourage freer and more outspoken media, especially the press. This will not only contribute to better flows of information on the effects of government policy and action but will also stimulate debate, articulate new policy ideas, air criticism of the way existing policies work and bring to public attention the needs of vulnerable sections of the population as well as disaster situations that require public action. This should, in turn, help to encourage more aware and responsive government.

Fifth, greater transparency in the procedures of government, together with an independent press and public scrutiny, should help to expose corruption and discourage 'rent-seeking' activity in relation to both policy formation and implementation. The more clear, simple and public the procedures for deciding issues and allocating public resources, the less chance there will be for personal or special community gain by stealth or corruption.

Finally, market or quasi-market allocation policies may accompany the return of multi-party politics and improve incentives and economic allocation of resources. There is no inevitable link of this kind but opposition parties often claim to have an interest in less discretionary state systems of allocation, at least while they are in opposition, if not when they are actually in power. When in opposition, politicians will want to limit the advantages of incumbency with its monopolisation of the allocation of public and private resources. While they may feel differently when in power themselves, the prospect of a permanent opposition should maintain pressure for a more decentralised policy process.

There are two or three illustrative areas of policy which might be beneficially affected by more open government or by a return to multi-party elections, such as we have seen recently in Zambia. First, the prospects for a greater voice from the poor and from rural areas might generate more public investment in rural health and education at the primary levels - a pattern of expenditure that seems to have a much higher rate of return than other forms of public expenditure. For example, there has been higher expenditure on public services in rural Botswana than in many other African economies, and this has been attributed to the more open political system and the desire to win rural votes.

Second, while greater scope for public pressures on the part of organised domestic business and labour interests (in non-export industries) may encourage protectionist trade policy, experience suggests that, once decisions have been taken to initiate policy reform, bold visible measures, which are announced in advance and publicly justified, seem most likely to ensure successful implementation of such reform (World Bank, 1989d).

Third, policy relating to pricing systems, especially agricultural pricing and marketing, has been weak and ineffective in many African countries. It is plausible to think that if there had been more rural and smallholder political expression in the 1970s, the pricing system and public services might have been more favourable to rural rather than urban interests.

Potential areas of tension

While political liberalisation and more 'inclusive' politics should help (perhaps only marginally) to re-establish or maintain more integrated societies, territorial sovereignty, greater law and order, and political stability, they may conflict with the pre-requisites of more effective economic management. There is an economic *quid pro quo* for more consensual politics in the form of greater ethnic accommodation and raised popular expectations. Thus there are some potential incompatibilities which experience elsewhere in the developing world appears to reinforce.

First, African economic policies were essentially short-term in orientation during the 1970s and early 1980s. Policy configuration often strongly reflected the self-interest of the ruling groups and their supporters. Yet wider political representation and increased openness seem unlikely to encourage the development of the types of longer-term strategies which have generally been lacking to date. Key features of the successful economic strategies of both Taiwan and South Korea, for example, were the commitment of the state elites to a clear ideology of long-term industrialisation, combined with an authoritarian system of rule which suppressed the emergence of independent interest groups and dampened pluralist pressures. If sub-Saharan Africa, which needs to encourage rather than suppress pluralism, has anything to learn from East Asia, it would seem to be the need for the state to have a clear vision of the national interest - an ideology for development - which provides a framework for longer-term economic and social perspectives while at the same time responding to and containing the pluralist pressures that democracy generates on the way. In improving the strategic dimension of economic policy in a more pluralist society, a key requirement is a bureaucracy of integrity and professional calibre and which is independent of sectional interests. As we have seen, it is a well recognised feature of the sub-Saharan African scene that the bureaucracies in many cases have been too closely involved in patrimonial politics, and have lacked independence and technical efficiency in offering advice on strategy, policy options and critical feedback to political leaders. Political leaders rarely seem to have encouraged the development of independent and scrupulous bureaucracies.

Second, maintaining an effective exchange-rate policy - a key issue in any economy - poses particular problems in a democracy because of its widespread impact, especially on real wages. Colombia has been a rarity in that the exchange rate was well managed in the context of democratic politics, while in the East Asian countries the maintenance of a competitive exchange rate is seen as a function of the 'insulation' of the responsible institutions as much as of the authoritarian system (Kahler, 1990). Jamaica illustrates the difficulty of reducing real wages and improving economic competitiveness via devaluation within a liberal democratic framework.

Another area of policy formation, which may be vulnerable to the pressures generated by more open and participatory politics, concerns the allocation of public expenditure and of financial resources, especially domestic credit and foreign exchange. Observers have attributed much responsibility for inappropriate allocation of public and private sector resources to systems of political patronage, which result in unwarranted interference in economic policy decisions and administered rather than price-determined allocations of credit and foreign exchange. In the periods of democratic transition there will remain strong - perhaps even stronger - pressures on political leaders to respond in the ways they have done in the past. The introduction of market-based allocation systems, which has occurred to some extent in recent years, will help to limit the politicisation of essentially financial and economic decisions which, when decentralised, seem more likely to improve the allocation and rates of return on invested funds. However, for this decentralisation to occur there must be continual societal pressure to deregulate and decontrol. This will depend very much on how independent economic interests organise and articulate their preferences in a more politically liberal system. In any case, a major role will remain for the public sector. The allocation of public resources and the management of public services will be prominent fields in which the new political rules of the game will be tested out.

Finally, there is the likelihood of increased strains on overall public budgetary control which may accompany distributional pressures on the executive in a more open political system. Budgetary control has been a weak element in most African countries during the last decade or more, and recourse to borrowing from the banking system, with consequent implications for the money supply, prices and competitiveness, has been a recurrent feature. The large, chronic fiscal deficits have been partly attributed to the politics of patronage, but there must be a worry that, when this narrow political support base is replaced by the need to respond to a much wider range of constituencies and pressures, the new political leadership will not have the will or experience to limit its response. While a number of African governments (both democratic and authoritarian) have made a series of 'technocratic' political appointments to Central Banks and Finance Ministries, it is quite plausible that more populist politics may once again emerge under a more liberal system (as it did in many countries at the time of independence) and that rash promises which have implications for public spending may be made by all political groupings to buy electoral support. Control over fiscal deficits, and hence control over inflation, has proved difficult in developing countries which have made the transition to democracy, particularly those where initial inflation was very high and politics were polarised. An archetypal example of this was the Garcia Government in Peru in the mid-1980s. This does not augur well for many African countries currently undergoing a process of democratisation, particularly those with divided societies.

This tension would seem a critical challenge which must be addressed in sub-Saharan Africa over the next decade if a process of political liberalisation and democratisation is to be reconciled with effective economic management. Careful thought must be given to what can be done to balance the desirable impetus towards a more 'inclusive' politics with the right degree of autonomy in state policy-making. If more consensual and inclusive politics involves some allocation of public resources to lower priority economic uses, this may well be an acceptable trade-off. However, there must be firm constraint on total budgets.

In any transition to more politically accountable government in Africa a high priority would be either some political insulation or much greater autonomy for the institutions which control bank lending to finance government deficits, or some respected statutory rules or limits on the scale of budget deficit which any legitimate or elected regime can operate. Under such circumstances, constitutional change to facilitate greater political liberalisation might have to be paralleled by some constitutional limits on the power of the executive to finance or monetise fiscal deficits. However, 'balanced budget' statutes have been more often a symbol of a basically conservative fiscal culture rather than an effective restraint *per se* on a spendthrift government. Increasing the independence of central banks is another option, though some would prefer a stronger coalition between the Ministry of Finance and the Central Bank to restrain spending pressures from the sectoral ministries. An important institutional reform is to strengthen budgetary accounting and audit procedures and systems so that governments actually know what they are doing with their expenditure both *ex ante* and *ex post*. These reforms need to accompany any political change of the kind envisaged here.

On balance where does this leave us? Certainly there can be no assurance that political liberalisation or multi-party democracy will also ensure better economic management. Governments which no longer monopolise power and are obliged to be more responsive to the effects of their actions on their own citizens should, as a result, formulate policies which are better adapted to changing conditions and needs, and are more credible and workable. Nevertheless, such governments will have to negotiate conflicts of interest more openly and skilfully, and handle the pressure of increased popular expectations in the context of limited state resources. The prospect for a combination of greater political freedom and competition with improved economic management seems most likely under conditions where excessive expectations are not encouraged, where the skills and morale of the bureaucracy can be rapidly improved, and where those who hold power seek institutional mechanisms effectively to control overall public expenditure or its monetary financing.

As Dunn has reminded us, 'The presence or absence of effectively guaranteed civil and political liberties does not in itself ensure the prevalence of good or bad government,' (1986:169). It is as well to remind ourselves of this to avoid disappointed expectations.

Annex 1

Glossary of Concepts and Terms in Political Science †

Contents

† Terms which appear frequently in the main text are listed in alphabetical order. Where other terms are given in bold these are explained either in the accompanying text or elsewhere in the glossary.

Accountability

1. Accountability concerns the sharing of the control and purposes of political power and implies a relation of reciprocity between the rulers and the ruled; it is not confined to constitutional devices which formally hold rulers to account for their actions, but is part of the wider social fabric of society.
2. The concept of accountability is embodied in the relation between the **state** and **civil society**; it is a function of the ability of interest groups and associations within civil society to curb the **hegemony** of the state.
3. Accountability is distinct from responsibility in that chains of responsibility run downwards by delegation, whereas chains of accountability run upwards by representation. Effective political representation is therefore equated with, but not identical to, political accountability.

Authoritarianism

1. Advocacy of **government** based on an established system of authority, rather than on consent. It is founded on the beliefs that a) people need authority and b) authority is not the outcome but the pre-condition of consent.
2. Authoritarianism also defines a particular form of **regime**, or philosophy that advocates such a form, where rulers impose their values on society by force irrespective of people's wishes. It includes fascism, communism, military dictatorships and most single-party regimes.
3. Bureaucratic authoritarianism is a political system where rules and regulations are implemented by a trained hierarchy of professionals in alliance with military or civilian rulers who are not subject to public **accountability**. Populist authoritarianism is sometimes used to describe a form of authoritarian rule which permits controlled mobilisation in support of a populist political agenda.
4. It contrasts with **paternalism** which is a benign system of traditional authority founded on norms and codes of conduct defined by hereditary rule.

Civil society

1. Originally a generic term for society and the state. Now it refers to organisations and institutions in the contemporary social order which are separate from and find expression in their relationship to the **state**.

2. The state is identified with a legal and institutional apparatus, whereas civil society denotes patterns of association (such as interest groups, professional bodies, membership organisations) which are customary and spontaneous and not necessarily dependent on the law [see **INTEREST GROUPS**].

Clientelism

1. Term used to describe informal power relations between individuals or groups in unequal positions, based on the exchange of benefits i.e. patron-client relations.
2. Clientelism in traditional societies occurs where a person with higher status (the patron) takes advantage of their authority and resources to protect and benefit somebody with inferior status (the client) who reciprocates with support and services. **Patron-client relations** are based on vertical linkages of a personal and affective nature, where the patron relies on prestige and the client demonstrates gratitude and devotion.
3. In complex societies clientelism operates through more intricate horizontal relationships involving organisations. Patrons act as brokers who establish the connection between the central power which distributes the resources, and the masses who reciprocate. Patrons control political organisations and allocate public resources (employment, material and social benefits), while clients reciprocate with political support. This type of clientelism relies on a political machine led by a boss who plays the role of a broker and a political leader.
4. **Patronage** is defined as the power and the acknowledged right of a political authority to appoint people to positions of responsibility in line with its own opinion, preference or interest. The choice made by the authority is discretionary and is based on trust, loyalty and political affinity rather than on political skill.
5. Extended and uncontrolled patronage can lead to a misuse of public resources in the form of corruption. In degenerative political situations, the term **prebendalism** has been used to describe a pattern of competition for public resources where the state is at the centre for economic advancement, and state offices are used for the benefit of patrons and clients.

Corporatism

1. **Corporatism** refers to the incorporation of favoured groups in decision making processes, especially in the area of state intervention in the economy and social welfare, in which **interest groups**

representing economic producers and providers of services are given privileged access to an informal bargaining process over public policies. In exchange for this privileged position, interest groups guarantee the compliance of their members to the agreed policies.

2. In authoritarian regimes (especially in Latin America) corporatist institutions permit the disciplining and control of labour, while offering protection to national industrial interests from international competition. Associations deemed legitimate by the state act as intermediaries between the state and economic producers, but there are constraints on independent interest group activity.

Democracy

1. Literal meaning is rule by the people, rather than by any section, class or interest. It is synonymous with popular rule and as such it is distinct from rule by the one (**monarchy** and **autocracy**), or several (**aristocracy** and **oligarchy**) [see **REGIME**].
2. Democracy in the West was deeply contested and was the product of a process of struggle. It was concerned with fostering the **accountability** of rulers to their subjects through the introduction of checks on the arbitrary use of power, agreed rules and procedures, and a separation of powers between the executive and the legislature. At a later stage (as **liberal democracy**) it became linked with universal franchise, competitive elections and equality before the law, enshrined within a formal constitution.
3. With the struggles for independence in colonial states, democracy became associated with collective self-determination rather than with the actuality of self-government. New nations often declared themselves as democratic on achieving independence (people's democracies or republics).
4. **Liberal democracy** is a form of rule where the powers of government are limited by law and citizens enjoy freedom of association to compete for office in free elections at regular intervals. There is a distinction between **direct democracy** where all citizens participate in decision-making, and **representative democracy** where people elect representatives who then take decisions on their behalf.
5. There is a view that democracy is not confined to the political sphere; it can be extended into the economic and social spheres, to encompass production, property and class relations.

Liberal democrats want to preserve the boundary between the state and individual liberty and property, and emphasise capitalism's free market contractual relations as a model for, and prerequisite, of democratic political life.

Egalitarian democrats by contrast focus their attention on equity and social justice as a foundation for democracy.

6. The term **polyarchy** is sometimes used in preference to democracy to avoid Western normative overtones, in societies where there is a relatively egalitarian social structure and a high degree of political participation. It implies that political leaders are responsive to the majority of the citizenry by free and fair elections, freedom of thought and organisation, the possibility of a legal opposition, a separation of powers with an independent judiciary and the institutionalised rule of law.
7. The degree of democracy is a function of the extent to which the political power of the elite is minimised and that of the non-elite maximised. It can be measured on the basis of the indicators of political liberties (press freedom, freedom of group opposition, government sanctions or ability to curtail political activities) and of popular sovereignty, which includes the fairness of elections, and the processes of executive and legislative selection.
8. Democratic transition (or **democratisation**) is used to describe the process by which countries move from authoritarian rule to democracy. This involves the creation of appropriate institutions, agreement over rules and procedures, and constitutional guarantees over basic political freedoms.

Government

1. The exercise of influence and control, through law and coercion, over a political community, constituted into a state within a defined territory.
2. An earlier, more restricted, definition divided government into three components: the **legislature** (which formulates policy and enacts it in law); the **executive** (which carries policy into action); and the **judiciary** (which applies the law according to the principles of procedural justice).
3. In most contemporary **liberal democracies** the judiciary is technically independent of government. Policy-making is the responsibility of the executive and policies are implemented by the civil service **bureaucracy**. The legislature debates and modifies policies before enacting them as law, but has limited influence over agenda-setting and policy formulation.
4. **Governance** refers to the use of legitimate authority exercised in the application of government power and in the management of public

affairs [see **LEGITIMACY**]. It is embodied in institutional arrangements, consultative mechanisms, policy-making processes and the nature and style of leadership in a political system.

5. **Good government** implies a high level of organisational effectiveness in relation to policy formulation and the policies actually pursued, especially in the conduct of economic policy and its contribution to growth, stability and popular welfare. Good government also implies **accountability, transparency, participation, openness** and the rule of law. It does not necessarily presuppose a value judgement about moral attributes of a **regime**, demonstrated, for example, in a healthy respect for civil and political liberties, although good government tends to be a prerequisite for political **legitimacy**.
6. **Openness** suggests that policies are generally subject to prior consultation and public discussion and that there is a legally enforceable right of public access to government records (i.e. freedom of information), the publicising of government functions and the right of the public to attend meetings of various government bodies. **Transparency** implies that government procedures are widely understood and decisions concerning the use of public resources are subject to scrutiny.

Hegemony

1. Hegemony refers to the political domination of one state over another, backed up, where necessary, by the use of force.
2. More dynamically, the term hegemony denotes ascendancy of a class, not only in the economic sphere, but also in the social, political and ideological spheres. Cultural supremacy is exercised through **civil society** (which includes mechanisms of socialisation such as the media, trade unions and the churches).

Ideology

1. **Ideologies** are patterns of beliefs and expressions that people use to interpret and evaluate the world in a way designed to shape, mobilise, direct, organise and justify certain modes and courses of action. In political theory ideology stands for all systems of ideas which find expression as political doctrines.
2. A **consensus** represents a set of beliefs, values and norms shared by individuals living in a given geographical unit at a given time. The functioning of consensus depends on three factors: a common acceptance of laws, rule and norms; an attachment to the institutions which promulgate and apply these laws and rules; a wide-

spread sense of unity or identity. Consensus over rules and procedures is a pre-requisite for the orderly and peaceful conduct of political affairs.

Interest groups

1. Interest groups are organisations within **civil society** which attempt to influence the direction of government policy without necessarily seeking political office. They are treated as a mechanism by which a diverse range of views can be absorbed into the democratic process, and are regarded as integral to **pluralism** since they provide a link between individuals and the state.
2. A distinction is sometimes made between 'insider' groups which are regularly consulted by government and are active in policy formation and implementation, and 'outsider' groups which are regarded as illegitimate by governments and struggle to influence the political agenda.
3. A distinction is sometimes made between groups which defend a particular sectional interest (farmers or trade unions), and those which seek to promote a specific political cause (pressure groups). In developing countries there is a further distinction between 'traditional' interest groups based on ascriptive ties (caste and ethnic associations) and 'modern' interest groups which have economic or class foundations.
4. In certain situations, interest groups participate in broader social movements, which are motivated by a degree of self-generated and independent action, leadership, and a minimal degree of organisation and participation on the part of the members of a group. Their activities are governed by new or emergent social and political norms rather than by existing customs and rules.

Legitimacy

1. The concept of legitimacy is essentially concerned with power and right. It emphasises the agency of the **state**, i.e. what gives the state the right to exercise power over its citizens, and the extent to which these powers are perceived to be rightly exercised.
2. In traditional society power was legitimised by divine or hereditary authority. In modern society the state derives legitimacy from the social acceptance of government authority. Legitimacy depends on the tacit assent of the governed, and a state is only legitimate to the extent that its subjects perceive it to be so.
3. Legitimate political representation is a function of a) the nature of the relationship between the state and **civil society** (which in turn

depends on the existence of a sentimental attachment to the nation-state, and the degree to which the state promotes people's needs and interests); b) the effectiveness of **government** (i.e. the skill and will with which it governs).

Pluralism

1. As an ideology pluralism recognises no single account as the ideal or absolute truth.
2. Political pluralism accepts a diversity of associations which funnel a diverse set of concerns, values and interests to the **state** for deliberation and resolution. It is also associated with a belief in the distribution of political power through several institutions which limit one another's action. Since it is premised on dispersed decision-making, political pluralism is associated with political stability where plural institutions perform a mediating role.
3. Various elements in the pluralist conception of politics include: an appreciation and respect for diversity (social customs, religious and moral beliefs and habits of association), protection of individual rights, political openness and creativity of politics, active citizenship, and a quest for consensus on common aims. By extension, a plural society is where diverse groups peaceably co-exist.

Populism

1. Populism is an approach to politics based on a direct appeal to 'the people', usually against the elite. It is used by charismatic rulers to circumvent conventional politics and entrenched political interests (for example in the bureaucracy) through an appeal based on the satisfaction of immediate material needs rather than on ideological commitment. In its more extreme form (in which it is closer to fascism), populism is a strategy designed to cultivate political support by blaming the ills that a society faces on outsiders or foreigners.
2. The **popular sector** is used as a shorthand for the labouring mass of the population (industrial workers, peasants, marginalised ethnic groups), which is perceived to share common political interests by virtue of its exclusion from mainstream politics and economic marginalisation.

Regime

1. A regime denotes a form of rule which is determined by the actual holders of office within **government** and operates on the basis of established procedures and institutional arrangements for the management of public affairs. A regime is a more durable form of

political organisation than a specific government, but is generally less permanent than a state. Hence a government may change, for example through defeat in an electoral contest, but the character of the regime (e.g. liberal democratic) can remain intact.

2. The character of a regime is determined by five basic elements:
   - Who rules? Individual or group, civilian or military control of executive authority?
   - Within what limits and what scope? Degree of responsiveness to popular pressure, power to enforce dictates.
   - In the name of what ends? Its ideological orientation.
   - By direct or individual means? Does its source of legitimacy stem directly from the people or is it subject to the will of a personal ruler?
   - Under what conditions and constraints? How far do economic or geo-political factors shape the form of the regime?
3. **Personal rule** is a political system dominated by strong personalised leadership where individuals and factions struggle for power, rather than over the right to govern. It is invariably grounded in **clientelism** which links rulers with patrons, clients, supporters and rivals through reciprocity, rather than through formal political institutions.
4. **Patrimonial rule** is a form of personal rule, where the right to rule is hereditary and conferred by tradition. A **monarchy** is where there is a sole hereditary head of state, whether titular or ruling.
5. An **autocracy** is where absolute power is in the hands of a single individual, who may be a sovereign ruler. **Absolutism** is an extreme form of personal rule where power is exercised without restriction. Similarly, **tyranny** is a corrupt form of personal rule where an absolute ruler uses power arbitrarily and oppressively.
6. An **aristocracy** is rule by a nobility or a privileged class. An **oligarchy** is a corrupt form of aristocracy, where the supreme power of the state is concentrated in the hands of a small exclusive class. In a **plutocracy**, state power is exercised by the wealthy, or a class of rich men.
7. **Polyarchy** [see **DEMOCRACY**] means government by many persons, and finds expression in the institutions or political processes of modern **representative democracy**.

Social class

1. At one level social class is a concept which describes the divisions in society, on the basis of economically determined social relations rooted in the production and exchange of goods and services.

2. A second meaning of social class refers to the world of lived experience that defines how individuals see themselves and one another. Social class also denotes a level of action in various spheres of life as private individuals, consumers, workers, citizens and lifestyle; it also reflected in voting behaviour and how people organise politically.
3. The notion of class interests presupposes that social classes are identified with a specific set of social and material interests which find expression in a particular **ideology**. In this schema, the interests of labour conflict with those of capital giving rise to a transformatory process of class struggle.
4. The term **dominant class** is used to refer to a social class which is dominant politically by virtue of the power and prestige conferred by the ownership of land and capital, or by traditional status (caste, nobility).

State

1. At its simplest, a state is defined as an organisation which monopolises legitimate force over a given territory (Weber); it also presumes a stable relationship between a territory and a political community.
2. The modern state possesses four basic features. It is:
   - an association among people for the end of government
   - a legally constituted organisation
   - attached to a particular territory
   - a recognised entity in international law (as a nation-state)
3. States are associated with a set of institutions or an apparatus, which generally include some combination of the following:
   - executive
   - legislature
   - bureaucracy
   - judiciary
   - military/police
4. The boundaries between these institutions are not always clear-cut; the notion of the **separation of powers** is used in democratic political contexts to refer to a division of responsibility between the executive and the legislature on the one hand, and the judiciary and the executive on the other. In **authoritarian** states, the boundaries between these bodies is blurred and indistinct.
5. The functions of a state are embodied in its institutions, in that policy-making is the prerogative of **government**, policies are debated by the legislature, and implemented by the bureaucracy.

The powers of arbitration and coercion rest with the judiciary and law enforcement agencies. State functions are partly determined by **ideology** of the **regime**, which may favour a limited or an expanded role for the state.

6. Considered simply, there are two contrasting perspectives on the role of the state: liberals view the state as a neutral actor, arbitrating between contending **interest groups**; marxists consider the state to be executive arm of the ruling **class** which safeguards the capitalist system.
7. The **autonomy** of a state in relation to **civil society** is both a question of power (where it has the strength to make and enforce its own laws) and of authority (where it is regarded as a **legitimate** government in a particular territory). A state has **relative autonomy** when it is not subject to the dictates of a single class or interest group, but in following its own agenda, assumes the role of a dominant class.
8. The concept of the **soft state** (analogous to that of the **weak state)** is used to describe states which have little **legitimacy** from within **civil society**. Such states do not exercise effective control over the territory under their jurisdiction, and rely on coercion to secure compliance. **State decay** is characterised by economic decline, a misuse of resources, administrative inefficiency and an absence of legitimacy.

Annex 2
Implications for Research

The review highlighted a number of gaps in the literature where there appears to be scope for further research. These relate to the policy process, the nature and likely course of political liberalisation, and the political consequences of structural adjustment in Africa.

First, there exist few in-depth studies of economic policy-making in developing countries, particularly in Africa. It remains unclear how policy was effectively formulated, and how different actors influence policy. Further research is needed to determine the nature of the decision-making process and the obstacles to effective policy-making in order to highlight possibilities for capacity-building initiatives. There is room for more case studies of how policy change was initiated, how it was designed, on what criteria and in response to what pressures, and why policy is more responsive to changing conditions in some countries than others. Also useful would be case studies of how specific policies were implemented, covering the relative influence of historical factors, political leadership, ideology, bureaucratic politics, patronage, technical analysis, pressures from interest groups and external agencies.

Comparative studies of the institutional and procedural context of policy-making and implementation in established democracies in the developing world (such as Jamaica, Mauritius, India, Costa Rica, Colombia), focusing on the mechanisms for consultation with interest groups would also be useful, particularly in comparison with non-democratic countries. Of particular interest are the extent and method of achieving consensus among different interest groups, and the degree to which policy initiatives are open to public scrutiny and critical feedback. The experience of policy consultation in developed countries would also be of interest, with a view to identifying the degree to which this experience is transferable. There is also scope for more comparative research of a kind which tests the hypothesis, that in more open politically competitive societies, the policy agenda is wider and the state formulates more workable and acceptable policies.

Second, the current wave of political reforms under way in parts of Africa has prompted much speculation about their characteristics and likely sustainability. Although a number of regimes are now formally committed to introducing multi-party structures, it is evident that a range of other political and institutional changes are also possible, particularly in countries resistant to dismantling the one-party structure or lacking basic political institutions. There is a need for more detailed research into the source of pressures (internal and external) for political liberalisation in Africa, the response of authoritarian regimes to such pressures, the institutional arrangements that have been developed to facilitate transition from authoritarian rule, and the nature of changes within one-party regimes which promote greater accountability and enhance their legitimacy. Research into the linkages between societal changes and pressures for democratisation would provide a more substantial underpinning to descriptions of the process of political reform, and provide the basis for a more penetrating assessment of the different actors involved and their principal motives.

Third, decentralisation has been highlighted in the literature as one possible means of achieving a greater dispersal of political power and of encouraging more local participation in decision-making. Some comparative research is already under way which explores this theme but there have been few detailed studies of local government and the process of decentralisation in sub-Saharan Africa. The political implications of such reforms as well as their effects on economic policy-making are both of interest and could benefit from further research.

Fourth, the literature on the composition and functioning of African bureaucracies is poorly-developed. There are few in-depth historical or comparative studies of bureaucracies which address their effectiveness, freedom for manoeuvre, capacity for independent decision-making, internal management, etc. Without such studies it is difficult to formulate proposals for administrative reform and better government.

Fifth, there seems to be a dearth of case studies in Africa which examine organised interest groups such as industrial, trading and business associations, farmers' organisations, professional bodies, trade unions, community groups and their role in influencing or checking state action. Some work in Africa tends to infer the pattern of political pressure from the character of emerging policy, yet it remains somewhat ambiguous how powerful or weak different interest groups are. The need is for empirical case studies which explore the resources, origins, tactics and operations of economic interest groups and their influence on state policy and practice, and the role of such groups in promoting greater participation in policy-making and implementation, all of which could encourage state responsiveness and more effectively designed and executed policies.

Finally, there has been little attention devoted to the political implications of economic reform. There has been some speculation that some changes in economic policy (e.g. bringing budgets under greater control and introducing more market-orientated allocation systems) could centralise political power, undermine political patronage systems or generate political unrest among those disadvantaged by the reforms. Such responses could in turn result in greater repression or more concerted attempts to mobilise grassroots party support by the political leadership. All of these processes could benefit from further in-depth studies. With current pressures for political change in Africa, research could also seek to test the hypothesis that political liberalisation and democratisation, through increased accountability and participation, is conducive to improved policy-making and the management of economic reform.

Bibliography

Abernethy, D.B. (1988), 'Bureaucratic Growth and Economic Stagnation in sub-Saharan Africa', in Commins.

Abernethy, D.B. (1989), 'The Influence of Aid Agencies on African Development: Recent Trends, Future Prospects', in Carter Center.

Ahmad, E., Drèze, J., Hills, J. and Sen, A. (1991), *Social Security in Developing Countries*. Oxford: Clarendon Press.

Ake, C. (1984), 'Ideology in Tanzania and Kenya', in Barkan.

Ake, C. (1990), 'The Case for Democracy', in Carter Center.

Almond, G. and Coleman, J.S. (eds) (1971), *The Politics of Developing Areas*. Princeton NJ: Princeton University Press.

Amin, S. (1987), 'Democracy and National Strategy in the Periphery', *Third World Quarterly*, 9 (4), 1129-1156.

Anderson, D. (1987), *Public Revenue and Economic Policy in African Countries*. Washington DC: World Bank, WPS 5.

Apter, D.E. (1963) (rev. edn), *Ghana in Transition*. Princeton NJ: Princeton University Press.

Apter, D.E. (1965), *The Politics of Modernization*. Chicago IL: Chicago University Press.

Arhink, K., Hesp, P. and van der Lann, L. (1986), *Marketing Boards in Tropical Africa*. London: Kegan Paul.

Armstrong, G. (1986), 'Whither Public Sector Institutional Development in Sub-Saharan Africa' (mimeo).

Austin, D. and Luckham, R. (eds) (1975), *Politicians and Soldiers in Ghana, 1966-72*. London: Frank Cass.

Azarya, V. (1988), 'Reordering State-Society Relations: Incorporation and Disengagement', in Rothchild and Chazan.

Bakary, T.D. (1990), 'Single Party Competitive Elections and Prospects for Democracy', in Carter Center.

Balassa, B. (1989), *Adjustment Policies in East Asia*, Washington DC: World Bank, Working Paper, WPS 280.

Bangura, V. (1988), 'The Crisis of Underdevelopment and the Transition to Civil Rule: Nigeria', *Africa Development*, 13 (1), 33-50.

Bardhan, P.K. (1984), *The Political Economy of Development in India*. Oxford: Blackwell.

Barkan, J. (ed.) (1984), *Politics and Public Policy in Kenya and Tanzania*. New York, Praeger.

Barro, R.J. (1991), 'Economic Growth in a Cross-section of Countries', *Quarterly Journal of Economics*, May.

Bates, R.H. (1981), *Markets and States in Tropical Africa*. Berkeley CA: University of California Press.

Bates, R.H. (1988), 'Political Basis for Agricultural Policy Reform', in Commins.

Bayart, J.P. (1986), 'Civil Society in Africa', in Chabal.

Berg-Schlosser, D. (1984), 'African Political Systems: Typology and Performance', *Comparative Political Studies*, 17 (1), 121-151.

Berg-Schlosser, D. (1989), 'Political System-Types as Determinants of Economic and Social Development in Africa - Comparative Case Studies', *Law and State*, 40, 88-119.

Bery, S.K. (1990), 'Economic Policy Reform in Developing Countries', *World Development*, 18 (8), 1123-1131.

Bienen, H. (1978), *Armies and Politics in Africa*. London: Africana.

Bienen, H. (1985), *Political Conflict and Economic Change in Nigeria*, London: Frank Cass.

Bienen, H. (1990), 'Politics of Trade Liberalization in Africa', *Economic Development and Cultural Change*, 38 (4), 713-732.

Bierstecker, T. (1990), 'Relations of Political and Economic Reforms, Structural Adjustment and Political Transition in Nigeria' (mimeo).

Binder, L. (1965), 'National Integration and Political Development', *American Political Science Review*, 58 (3), April, 622-631.

Bollen, K.A. (1980), 'Issues in the Comparative Measurement of Political Democracy', *American Sociological Review*, 45, June, 370-390.

Bollen, K. and Grandjean, B.D. (1981), 'Dimensions of Democracy: Future Issues in Measurement and Effects of Political Democracy', *American Sociological Review*, 46, October, 651-659.

Bollen, K. and Jackman, R. (1985), 'Political Democracy and the Size Distribution of Income', *American Sociological Review*, 50.

Booth, D. (1987), 'Alternatives for Restructuring State Society Relations: Research Issues in Tropical Africa', *IDS Bulletin*, 18 (4), 23-30.

Bowman, L.W. (1991), *Mauritius: Democracy and Development in the Indian Ocean*. Boulder CO & London: Westview.

Bratton, M. (1989), 'Beyond Autocracy: Civil Society in Africa', in Carter Center.

Brett, E.A. (1973), *Colonialism and Underdevelopment in East Africa: The Politics of Economic Change 1919-1939*. London: Heinemann.

Brough, W.T. and Kimanyi, M.S. (1986), 'On the Inefficient Extraction of Rents by Dictators', *Public Choice*, 48 (1), 37-48.

Callaghy, T.M. (1986), 'Politics and Vision in Africa: The Interplay of Domination, Equality and Liberty', in Chabal.

Callaghy, T.M. (1988), 'The State and the Development of Capitalism in Africa: Theoretical, Historical and Comparative Reflections', in Rothchild and Chazan.

Callaghy, T.M. (1990), 'Lost Between State and Market: The Politics of Adjustment in Ghana, Zambia and Nigeria', in Nelson.

Cardoso, F.H. (1979), 'On the Characterization of Authoritarian Regimes in Latin America', in Collier.

Carter Center (1989), *Beyond Autocracy in Africa*, Working Paper Series.

Carter Center (1990), *African Governance in the 1990s*, Working Paper Series.

Carter Center (1991), *Africa Demos*, 1 (4), May.

Cartwright, J. (1983), *Political Leadership in Africa*. London: Croom Helm.

Cavarozzi, M. (1986), 'Political Cycles in Argentina since 1955', in O'Donnell *et al.*, Vol. II, *Latin America*.

Chabal, P. (ed.) (1986), *Political Domination in Africa: Reflections on the Limits of Power*. Cambridge: Cambridge University Press.

Chalker, L. (1991), 'Good Government and the Aid Programme', Speech to ODI/Chatham House, 25 June.

Chazan, N. (1982), 'The New Politics of Participation in Tropical Africa,' *Comparative Politics*, 14 (2), 169-190.

Chazan, N. (1988a), 'Ghana: Problems of Governance and the Emergence of Civil Society', in Diamond *et al.*, Vol. II, *Africa*.

Chazan, N. (1988b), 'Patterns of State-Society Incorporation and Disengagement in Africa', in Rothchild and Chazan.

Chazan, N. and Rothchild, D. (eds) (1988), *The Precarious Balance: State and Society in Africa*. Boulder CO and London: Westview.

Cohen, Y. (1985), 'Impact of Bureaucratic Authoritarian Rule on Economic Growth', *Comparative Political Studies*, 18, 123-136.

Colclough, C. and Manor, J. (eds) (1991), *States or Markets: Neo-Liberalism and the Development Policy Debate*. Oxford: Oxford University Press.

Coleman, J.S. (1971), 'The Political Systems of Developing Areas', in Almond and Coleman.

Coleman, J.S. and Rosberg, C.G. (1964), *Political Parties and National Integration in Tropical Africa*. Berkeley and Los Angeles CA: University of California Press.

Collander, D. (ed.) (1984), *Neo-Classical Political Economy: The Analysis of Rent Seeking and Directly Unproductive Activities*. Cambridge MA:

Ballinger.

Collier, D. (ed.) (1979a), *The New Authoritarianism in Latin America*. Princeton NJ: Princeton University Press.

Collier, D. (1979b), 'Overview of the Bureaucratic-Authoritarian Model', in Collier.

Collier, R.B. (1982), *Regimes in Tropical Africa: Changing Forms of Supremacy, 1945-1975*. Berkeley and Los Angeles CA: University of California Press.

Commins, S.K. (1988), *African Development Challenges and the World Bank: Hard Questions and Costly Choices*. Boulder CO: Lynne Rienner.

Coulon, C. (1988), 'Senegal: The Development and Fragility of Semidemocracy', in Diamond *et al.*, Vol. II, *Africa*.

Crook, R. (1989), 'Patrimonialism, Administrative Effectiveness and Economic Development in Côte d'Ivoire', *African Affairs*, 88 (351), 205-229.

Crook, R.C. (1988), 'State Capacity and Economic Development: Côte d'Ivoire', *IDS Bulletin*, 19 (4), 19-25.

Crowder, M. (1987), 'Whose Dream was it Anyway? Twenty-five Years of African Independence', *African Affairs*, 86 (342), January, 7-24.

Cruise O'Brien, D.B. (1978), 'Senegal', in Dunn.

Dahl, R.A. (1971), *Polyarchy*, New Haven CT: Yale University Press.

Deaton, A. (1990) *Savings in Developing Countries, Theory and Review*. Washington DC: World Bank, RDPS Discussion Paper 144.

Decalo, S. (1976), *Coups and Army Rule in Africa: Studies in Military Style*. New Haven CT: Yale University Press.

Decalo, S. (1985), 'African Personal Dictatorships', *Journal of Modern African Studies*, 23 (2), 209-237.

Diamond, L. (1987), 'Class Formation in The Swollen African State', *Journal of Modern African Studies*, 25 (4), 567-596.

Diamond, L. (1988a), 'Introduction: Roots of Failure, Seeds of Hope', in Diamond *et al.*, Vol. II, *Africa*.

Diamond, L. (1988b), 'Nigeria: Pluralism, Statism, and the Struggle for Democracy', in Diamond *et al.*, Vol. II, *Africa*.

Diamond, L. and Linz, J.J. (1989), 'Introduction: Politics, Society and Democracy in Latin America', in Diamond *et al.*, Vol. IV, *Latin America*.

Diamond, L., Linz, J.J. and Lipset, S.M. (eds) (1988), *Democracy in Developing Countries;* Vol. II, *Africa*. Boulder CO: Lynne Rienner.

Diamond, L., Linz, J.J. and Lipset, S.M. (eds) (1989), *Democracy in*

Developing Countries, Vol. IV, *Latin America*, Boulder CO: Lynne Rienner.

Doornbos, M. (1990), 'The African State in Academic Debate: Retrospect and Prospect', *Journal of Modern African Studies*, 28 (2), June, 177-198.

Dornbusch, R. and Edwards, S. (1989), *Macro-Economics of Populism in Latin America*. Washington DC: World Bank, WPS 316.

Drèze, J. and Sen, A. (1991), 'Public Action for Social Security: Foundation and Strategy', in Ahmad *et al.*

Duignan, P. and Jackson, R.H. (eds) (1986), *Politics and Government in African States, 1960-85*. London: Croom Helm.

Dunn, J. (1986), 'The Politics of Representation and Good Government in Post-Colonial Africa', in Chabal.

Dunn, J. (ed.) (1978), *West African States: Failure and Promise*, Cambridge: Cambridge University Press.

Dutkierwicz, P. and Williams, G. (1987), 'All the King's Horses...', *IDS Bulletin*, 18 (3), 39-44.

Easterly, W.R. and Witzel, D. (1989), *Policy Determinants of Growth*. Washington DC: World Bank, WPS 343.

Edwards, S. and Tabellini, G. (1991), 'The Political Economy of Fiscal Policy and Inflation in Developing Countries'. Washington DC: World Bank, WPS 703.

Ellis, S. (1991), 'Governance in French-Speaking Africa', Paper Presented at a Conference Sponsored by Queen Elizabeth House, University of Oxford and the World Bank, Washington D.C. on Governance and Economic Development in sub-Saharan Africa, May.

Ergas, Z. (1986), 'In Search of Development', *Journal of Modern African Studies*, 24 (2), 303-334.

Ethier, D. (1990a), 'Processes of Transition and Democratic Consolidation: Theoretical Indicators', in Ethier.

Ethier, D. (ed.) (1990b), *Democratic Transition and Consolidation in Southern Europe, Latin America and Southeast Asia*. London: Macmillan.

Evans, P. (1979), *Dependent Development: The Alliance of Multinational, State and Local Capital in Brazil*. Princeton NJ: Princeton University Press.

Fearon, J.D. (1988), 'International Financial Institutions and Economic Policy Reform in Sub-Saharan Africa', *Journal of Modern African Studies*, 26 (1), 113-137.

Findlay, R. (1989), *Is the New Political Economy Relevant to Developing*

Countries? Washington DC: World Bank, WPS 292.

Friedman, M. (1962), *Capitalism and Freedom*. Chicago IL: University of Chicago Press.

Friedman, M. (1980), *Free to Choose*. New York: Harcourt Brace Jovanovich.

Garrity, M. and Picard, L.A. (1991), 'Organized Interests, the State, and the Public Policy Process', *Journal of Developing Areas*, 25 (3), April, 369-394.

Gastil, R.D. (1987), *Freedom in The World: Political Rights and Civil Liberties, 1986-1987*. New York: Greenwood.

Geertz, C. (1963), 'The Integrative Revolution: Primordial Sentiments and Civil Politics in the New States', in Geertz.

Geertz, C. (ed.) (1963), *Old Societies and New States: The Quest for Modernity in Asia and Africa*. New York: Doubleday.

Gelb, A. (1989), *A Cross Section Analysis of Financial Policies Efficiency and Growth*. Washington DC: World Bank, WPS 202.

Gertzel, C. *et al.* (1984), *Dynamics of The One Party State in Zambia*. Manchester: Manchester University Press.

Glentworth, G. and Sparkhall, K. (eds) (1989) *Civil Service Reform in Sub-Saharan Africa*. London: Overseas Development Administration (mimeo).

Gluckman, M. (1965), *Politics, Law and Ritual in Tribal Society*, Oxford: Blackwell.

Graf, W. (1988), 'Issues and Substance in the Prescription of Liberal - Democratic Forms for Nigeria's Third Republic,' *African Affairs*, 350, 91-100.

Graham, L.S. (1980), 'Democracy and the Bureaucratic State in Latin America', in Wiarda.

Green, R.H. and Colclough, C. (1988), 'Editorial Introduction', *IDS Bulletin*, 19 (1), January.

Grindle, M.S. (1989), *The New Political Economy: Positive Economics and Negative Politics*. Washington DC: World Bank, WPS 304.

Grindle, M.S. and Thomas, J.W. (1989), 'Policy Makers, Policy Choices, and Policy Outcomes: The Political Economy of Reform in Developing Countries', *Policy Sciences*, 22, 213-248.

Grindle, M.S. and Thomas, J.W. (1990), 'After the Decision: Implementing Policy Reforms in Developing Countries,' *World Development*, 18 (8), 1163-1181.

Gulhati, R. (1989), *Malawi: Promising Reforms Bad Luck*. Washington DC: World Bank. EDI Policy Case Study No. 3, Economic Development Institute.

Gulhati, R. (1990), *Zambia, The Economics and Politics of Reform.* Washington DC: World Bank. EDI Policy Case Study No. 2, Economic Development Institute.

Gutteridge, W.F. (1975), *Military Regimes in Africa.* London: Methuen.

Haggard, S., Kim, B.K. and Moon, C. (1990), *The Transition to Export Led Growth in South Korea, 1954-66.* Washington DC: World Bank, WPS 546.

Haggard, S. and Kaufman, R. (1990), *The Political Economy of Inflation and Stabilization in Middle Income Countries.* Washington DC: World Bank, WPS 444.

Harris, J. (1987), 'The State in Retreat? Why has India Experienced Half Hearted Liberalization?' *IDS Bulletin* 18 (4), 31-38.

Harris, P. (1986), 'Formulation of Public Policy in the Absence of Democracy', *International Political Science Review*, 7 (1), 82-90.

Harvey, C. (1990), *Recovery From Macro Economic Disaster in Africa*, IDS (mimeo).

Harvey, C. and Lewis, S.R. (1990), *Policy Choice and Development in Botswana.* London: Macmillan.

Hawthorn, G. (1991), 'Democracy and Good Government: How and Why African States Fall Short', Paper presented at the Oxford Conference on Governance and Economic Management in Sub-Saharan Africa.

Hecht, R. (1983), 'The Ivory Coast Miracle, What Benefits for the Farmers?', *Journal of Modern African Studies*, 21 (1), 25-53.

Helleiner, G.K. (ed.) (1986), *Africa and the International Monetary Fund.* Washington DC: IMF.

Herbst, J. (1989), 'Political Impediment to Economic Rationality: Explaining Zimbabwe's Failure to Reform its Public Sector', *Journal of Modern African Studies*, 27 (1), 67-84.

Herbst, J. (1990a), 'Migration, The Politics of Protest, and State Consolidation in Africa', *African Affairs*, 89 (335), April, 183-203.

Herbst, J. (1990b), 'Structural Adjustment of Politics in Africa', *World Development*, 18 (7), 949-958.

Heymans, C. (1986), 'The Politics of Accommodation in the Second Republic: An Analysis of Nigerian Democracy between 1979 & 83', *Africanus*, 16 (1-2), 18-27.

Hirschman, A.O. (1981), *Essays in Tresspassing: Economics to Politics and Beyond.* Cambridge: Cambridge University Press.

Hodd, M. (1987), 'Africa, the IMF and the World Bank', *African Affairs*, 86 (344), 331-342.

Hodder-Williams, R. (1984), *An Introduction to the Politics of Tropical*

Africa. London: Unwin Hyman.

Holm, J.D. (1988), 'Botswana: A Paternalistic Democracy', in Diamond *et al.*, Vol. II, *Africa*.

Holmquist, F. (1989), 'Why Democratic Forms of Rule in Africa are Necessary and Possible', in Carter Center.

Holt, R.T. (1966), *The Political Element in Economic Development*. Toronto: Van Nostrand.

Hopkins, R.F. (1979), 'The Influence of the Legislature on Development Strategy: The Case of Kenya and Tanzania', in Smith and Musolf.

Huntington, S.P. (1965), 'Political Development and Political Decay', *World Politics*, 18 (7), 286-330.

Huntington, S. (1984), 'Will Countries Become More Democratic?', *Political Science Quarterly*, 99 (2), Summer, 193-219.

Hurd, D. (1990), Speech to a Conference on 'Prospects for Africa in the 1990s' at the Overseas Development Institute, 6 June.

Hyden, G. (1983), *No Shortcuts to Progress*. Los Angeles CA: University of California Press.

Ihonvbere, J.O. and Ekekwe, E.N. (1988), 'Dependent Capitalism, Structural Adjustment and Democratic Possibilities: Nigeria's Third Republic', *Africa Spectrum*, 23 (3), 273-292.

Jackson, R.H. (1986), 'Conclusion', in Duignan and Jackson.

Jackson, R.H. and Rosberg, C.G. (1982), *Personal Rule in Black Africa: Prince, Autocrat, Prophet, Tyrant*. Berkeley CA: University of California Press.

Jackson. R.H. and Rosberg, C.G. (1988), 'Why Africa's Weak States Persist: The Empirical and the Juridical in Statehood', *World Politics*, 35, October, 1-24.

Joseph, R.A. (1983), 'Class, State and Prebendal Politics in Nigeria', *Journal of Commonwealth and Comparative Politics*, 21 (3).

Joseph, R.A. (1990), 'Partnership', *Africa Report*, July/August, 28-30.

Kahler, M. (1990), 'Orthodoxy and its Alternatives: Explaining Approaches to Stabilization and Adjustment', in Nelson.

Kasfir, N. (ed.) (1984), *State and Class in Africa*. London: Frank Cass.

Kasoma, F. (1980), 'The Role of the Press', in Woldring and Chibaye.

Ketley, R. (1991), 'Identifying the Links Between Political Regimes and Economic Management in Sub-Saharan Africa'. London: ODI (mimeo).

Killick, T. (1978), *Development Economics in Action, Ghana*. London: Heinemann.

Killick, T. (1989), 'Principles of Policy for the Adaptive Economy'.

Working Paper No. 32. London: Overseas Development Institute.

Killick, T. and Mwega, F.M. (1990), 'Monetary Policy in Kenya 1967-88'. *Working Paper No. 39*. London: Overseas Development Institute.

Kimenyi, M.S. (1985), 'Political Party Competition and Managerial Behaviour: An Issue Analysis in Parastatal Management', *East African Economic Review*, 1 (1), December 39-46.

King, D.Y. (1981), 'Regime Type and Performance', *Comparative Political Studies*, 13 (4), January, 478-505.

Kirk-Greene, A.H.M. (1991), 'His Eternity, His Eccentricity, or His Exemplarity: A Further Contribution to the Study of H.E. the African Head of State', *African Affairs*, 90 (350), 163-187.

Klitgaard, R. (1989), 'Incentive Myopia', *World Development*, 17 (4), 447-459.

Kohli, A. (ed.) (1986) *The State and Development in the Third World*, Princeton: Princeton University Press.

Kohli, A. (1989), 'Politics of Economic Liberalization in India', *World Development*, 17 (3), 305-328.

Krueger, A. (1974), 'Political Economy of the Rent Seeking Society', *American Economic Review*, 64 (3), 291-303.

Kwan, S.K. (1989), 'On the Political Economy of Export-Oriented Industrialization: Korea and Taiwan', *Economics*, 39.

Kunz, F.A. (1990), 'Liberalization in Africa - Some Preliminary Reflections', *African Affairs*, 90 (350), April, 223-235.

Kuznets, S. (1966), *Modern Economic Growth: Rate, Structure and Spread*. New Haven CT: Yale University Press.

Kydd, J. (1988), 'Policy Reform and Adjustment under Siege: Malawi, 1980-87', *IDS Bulletin*, 19 (1), 71-42.

Lal, D. (1987), 'Political Economy of Economic Liberalization', *World Bank Economic Review*, 1 (2), 273-301.

Lamb, G. (1987), *Managing Economic Policy Change: Institutional Dimensions*. Washington DC: World Bank, Discussion Paper No.14.

Lancaster, C. (1989), 'The Governance of Africa by Aid Donors', in Carter Center.

Landau, D. (1986), 'Government and Economic Growth in Less Developed Countries: An Empirical Study for 1960-1980', *Economic Development and Cultural Change*, 35 (1), October, 35-76.

Landell-Mills, P. and Serageldin, I. (1991), 'Governance and the External Factor'. Washington DC: World Bank, Annual Conference on Development Economics (mimeo).

Lane, C. (1989), 'Monetary Policy Effectiveness in Côte d'Ivoire'. *Working Paper No. 30*. London: Overseas Development Institute.

Lehmann, D. (ed.) (1979), *Development Theory: Four Critical Studies*. London: Frank Cass.

Lemarchand, R. (1988), 'The State, the Parallel Economy, and the Changing Structure of Patronage Systems', Rothchild and Chazan.

Leonard, D.K. (1987), 'Political Realities of African Management', *World Development*, 15 (7), 899-910.

LeVine, V.T. (1979), 'Parliaments in Francophone Africa', in Smith and Musolf.

Levy, D.C. (1989), 'Mexico: Sustained Civilian Rule Without Democracy', Diamond *et al.*, Vol. IV *Latin America*.

Leys, C. (1975), *Underdevelopment in Kenya: The Political Economy of Neo-Colonialism*. London: Heinemann.

Leys, C. (1976), 'The "Overdeveloped" Post-Colonial State: A Re-evaluation', *Review of African Political Economy*, January-April, 39-48.

Lindblom, C.E. (1977), *Politics and Markets*. New Haven CT: Yale University Press.

Linz, J.J. (1978), 'Crisis, Breakdown, and Re-equilibration', in Part I of Linz and Stepan.

Linz, J.J. and Stepan, A. (ed.) (1978), *The Breakdown of Democratic Regimes*. Baltimore MD: Johns Hopkins University Press.

Lipset, S.M. (1959), 'Some Social Requisites of Democracy: Economic Development and Political Legitimacy', *American Political Science Review*, 53, 69-105.

Lipset, S.M. (1960), *Political Man: The Social Basis of Politics*. London: Heineman.

Lonsdale, J. (1986) 'Political Accountability in African History', in Chabal.

Lonsdale, J. (1981), 'States and Social Processes in Africa: A Historiographical Survey', *African Studies Review*, 24 (2-3), 139.

Luckham, R. (1971), *The Nigerian Military: A Sociological Analysis of Authority and Revolt, 1960-67*. London: Cambridge University Press.

Luedde-Neurath, R. (1990), 'State Intervention and Export-Oriented Development in South Korea', in White and Wade.

Lukes, P.F. and Riley, S.P. (1989), 'Sierra Leone: The politics of Economic Decline', *Journal of Modern African Studies*, 27 (1), 133-141.

Lungu, G.F. (1986), 'Church, Labour and the Press in Zambia: The Role of Critical Observers in a One Party State', *African Affairs*, 85 (340), 385-410.

MacGaffey, J. (1987), *Entrepreneurs and Parasites: The Struggle for Indigenous Capitalism in Zaire*. Cambridge: Cambridge University Press.

Marsh, R.M. (1988), 'Sociological Explanations of Economic Growth', *Studies in Comparative International Research*, Winter, 41-75.

Martin, M. (1991), *The Crumbling Façade of African Debt Negotiations: No Winners*. London: Macmillan.

McGowan P. and Johnson J.H. (1985), 'Military Coup d'Etats and Underdevelopment', *Journal of Modern African Studies*, 22 (4), 633-667.

Molutsi, P.P. and Holm, J.D. (1990), 'Developing Democracy when Civil Society is Weak: The Case of Botswana', *African Affairs*, 89 (356), 323-340.

Momba, J.C. (1989), 'State, Class Formation and Political Participation in Zambia', *African Affairs*, July, 352.

Moore, B. (1966), *The Social Origins of Dictatorship and Democracy*. Harmondsworth: Penguin.

Moore, M. (1987), 'Interpreting Africa's Crisis', *IDS Bulletin*, 18 (4), 7-16.

Mosley, P. (1986), 'The Politics of Economic Liberalization: USAID and the IBRD in Kenya', *African Affairs*, 88 (338), 107-120.

Mosley, P., Toye, J. and Harrigan, J. (1991), *Aid and Power: The World Bank and Policy-based Lending*. 2 Vols. London: Routledge.

Mutahaba, G. (1990), 'Innovations in African Governance', in Carter Center.

Nabudere, D.W. (1989), 'The One-Party State in Africa and its Assumed Philosophical Roots', in Meyns and Nabudere.

Nelson, J.M. (1984), 'Political Economy of Stabilization, Commitment Capacity and Public Response', *World Development*, 12 (4), 983-1006.

Nelson, J.M. (1987), 'Political Participation', in Weiner and Huntington.

Nelson, J.M. (ed.) (1989), *Fragile Coalitions: The Politics of Adjustment in the Third World*. Washington DC. Overseas Development Council.

Nelson, J.M. (ed.) (1990), *Economic Crisis and Policy Choice: The Politics of Adjustment in the Third World*. Princeton NJ: Princeton University Press.

North, D.C. (1984), 'Three Approaches to the Study of Institutions', in Collander.

Nyang'oro, J.E. and Shaw, T.M. (eds) (1989), *Corporatism in Africa: Comparative Analysis and Practice*. Boulder CO, London and San Francisco : Westview.

Nyong'o, Anyang P. (1988), 'Political Instability and the Prospects for Democracy in Africa', *Africa Development*, 13 (1), 71-86.

Nyong'o, Anyang P. (1989), 'State and Society in Kenya', *African*

Affairs, 88 (351), 229-252.

O'Brien, D.C. (1979), 'Modernization, Order and the Erosion of a Democratic Ideal', in Lehmann.

O'Donnell, G. (1979), 'Tensions in the Bureaucratic-Authoritarian State and the Question of Democracy', in Collier.

O'Donnell, G. (1986), 'Introduction to the Latin American Cases', in O'Donnell *et al.*, Vol. II, *Latin America.*

O'Donnell, G., Schmitter, P. and Whitehead, L. (eds) (1986), *Transitions from Authoritarian Rule: Prospects for Democracy.* 4 Volumes. I. *Southern Europe*, II. *Latin America*, III. *Comparative Perspectives*, IV. *Tentative Conclusions About Uncertain Democracies.* Baltimore MD: Johns Hopkins University Press.

ODI (1992), 'Aid and Political Reform', ODI *Briefing Paper*. London: Overseas Development Institute; January.

Oyediran, O. and Agbaje, A. (1991), 'Two-Partyism and Democratic Transition in Nigeria', *Journal of Modern African Studies*, 29 (2), 213-235.

Oyugi, W.O. *et al.* (1988), *Democratic Theory and Practice in Africa.* London: James Currey.

Paul, S., Steedman, D. and Sutton F.C. (1989), *Building Capability for Policy Analysis.* Washington DC: World Bank, WPS 220.

Perfect, D. (1986), 'Organised Labour and Politics in The Gambia', *Labour, Capital and Society*, 19 (2), 168-199.

Post, K. (1968), *The New States of West Africa*, Harmondsworth: Penguin.

Pourgerami, A. (1988), 'The Political Economy of Development', *Public Choice*, 58, 123-141.

Pryor, F.L. (1991), *Malawi and Madagascar, The Political Economy of Poverty, Equality and Growth.* Oxford: Oxford University Press.

Ravenhill, J. (1980), 'Comparing Regime Performance in Africa: The Limits of Cross-National Aggregate Analysis', *Journal of Modern African Studies*, 10 (1), 99-126.

Remmer, K.L. (1986), 'Politics of Economic Stabilization in Latin America', *Comparative Politics*, 9, (1).

Remmer, K.L. (1990), 'Democracy and Economic Crisis', *World Politics*, 42, 315-335.

Rimmer, D. (1986), *Economics of West Africa.* London: Weidenfeld and Nicolson.

Rondinelli, D.A. (1986), 'Administration of Integrated Rural Development Policy: The Politics of Agrarian Reform in Developing Countries', in Kohli.

Rosberg, C. and Friedland, W.H. (1964), *African Socialism*, Stanford CA: Stanford University Press.

Rostow, W.W. (1971), *Politics and the Stages of Growth and Decline of Democracy*. London: Cambridge University Press.

Rothchild, D. and Chazan, N. (eds) (1988), *The Precarious Balance: State and Society in Africa*. Boulder CO and London: Westview.

Rothchild, D. and Foley, M.W. (1988), 'African States and the Politics of Inclusive Coalitions', in Rothchild and Chazan.

Rustow, D.A. (1970), 'Transitions to Democracy: Towards a Dynamic Model', *Comparative Politics*, 2 (3), April, 337-362.

Ruttan, V. (1991), 'What Happened to Political Development?', *Economic Development and Culture Change*, 39 (2), 269-292.

Sallah, T.M. (1990), 'Economics and Politics in The Gambia', *Journal of Modern African Studies*, 28 (4), 632-648.

Sandbrook, R.C. (1985), *The Politics of Africa's Economic Stagnation*. Cambridge: Cambridge University Press.

Sandbrook, R.C. (1986), 'The State and Economic Stagnation in Tropical Africa', *World Development*, 14 (3), 319-32.

Schumpeter, J. (1976), 5th Edition, *Capitalism, Socialism and Democracy*. New York: Harper.

Sen, A. (1983), 'Development: Which Way Now?', *Economic Journal*, 93, 745-762.

Shams, (1989), 'Adjustment Constraints in Developing Countries: A Comparative Study', *Intereconomics*, 24 (2), 71-78.

Sheahan, J. (1980), 'Market Oriented Policies and Political Repression', *Economic Development and Cultural Change*, 28 (2), 267-292.

Sirowy, L. and Inkeles, A. (1990), 'Effects of Democracy on Economic Growth and Inequality: A Review', *Studies in Comparative International Development*, 25 (1), 126-157.

Sissons, R. and Snowiss, L.M. (1979) 'Legislative Viability and Political Development', in Smith and Musolf.

Skålnes, T. (1989), 'Group Interests and the State: An Explanation of Zimbabwe's Agricultural Policies', *Journal of Modern African Studies*, 27 (1), March, 85-107.

Sklar, R.L. (1979), 'The Nature of Class Domination in Africa', *Journal of Modern African Studies*, 17 (4), December.

Sklar, R.L. (1986), 'Democracy in Africa', in Chabal.

Sklar, R.L. (1988), 'Beyond Capitalism and Socialism in Africa', *Journal of Modern African Studies*, 26 (1), 1-21.

Sloan, J. and Tedin, K.L. (1987), 'Consequences of Regime Type for Public Policy Outputs', *Comparative Political Studies*, 20 (1), April,

98-124.

Smith, J. and Musolf, L.D. (eds) (1979), *Legislatures and Development*. Durham NC: Duke University Press.

Somerville, K. (1991), 'Africa Moves Towards Party Pluralism', *The World Today*, August/September, 152-155.

Srinivasan, T.N. (1985), 'Neo-classical Political Economy: The State and Economic Development', *Asian Development Review*, 3 (2), 38-98.

Staniland, M. (1986), 'Democracy and Ethnocentrism', in Chabal.

Stark, F.M. (1986), 'Theories of Contemporary State Formation in Africa: A Reassessment', *Journal of Modern African Studies*, 24 (2), 335-347.

Stevens, C. and Speed, J. (1977), 'Multi-partyism in Africa: The Case of Botswana Revisited', *African Affairs*, 76 (304), July, 381-7.

Taylor, L. (1987), *Varieties of Stabilization Experience in the Third World*. Helsinki: WIDER.

Teal, F. (1988), 'Domestic Policies, External Constraints and Economic Development in Nigeria Since 1950', *African Affairs*, 87 (346), 69-82.

Terrell, K. and Suejnor, J. (1990), *How Industry/Labour Relations and Government Policies Affect Senegal's Economic Performance*. Washington DC: World Bank, WPS 271.

Tordoff, W. (1984), *Politics and Government in Africa*. London: Macmillan.

Toye, J. (1989), 'A Comment on Three Conceptual Papers by Grindle, Ranis and Findlay', Institute of Development Studies (mimeo).

Toye, J. (1990), 'Is There a New Political Economy of Development?', in Colclough and Manor.

Toye, J. (1991), 'Interest Group Politics and the Implementation of Adjustment Policies in Africa', IDS (mimeo).

UNDP (1991), *Human Development Report*, New York and Oxford: UNDP.

van Donge, J.K. and Liviga, A.J. (1986), 'Tanzanian Political Culture and the Cabinet', *Journal of Modern African Studies*, 24 (4), December, 619-64.

van Donge, J.K. and Liviga, A.K. (1989), 'The 1985 Tanzanian Parliamentary Elections: A Conservative Election', *African Affairs*, 88 (350), January, 47-62.

Vasant, J. (1989), 'Opportunities and Risks for Private Voluntary Organizations as Agents of LDC Policy Change', *World Development*, 17 (11), 1723-1732.

Wade, R. (1991), *Governing the Market: Economic Theory and the Role of*

Government in East Asian Industrialization. Princeton NJ: Princeton University Press.

Weede, E. (1983), 'Impact of Democracy on Economic Growth Some Evidence from Gross National Analysis', *Kyklos*, 36 (1), 21-39.

Weiner, M. and Huntington, S.P. (1987), *Understanding Political Development: An Analytical Study*. Glenview IL: Scott, Foresman and Co.

White, G. and Wade, R. (eds) (1990), *Development States of East Asia*. Brighton: Research Report, IDS.

Whitehead, L. (1990), 'Political Explanations of Macro-Economic Management: A Survey', *World Development*, 18 (8), 1133-1146.

Whitehead, L. (1989), 'Democratization and Disinflation', in Nelson.

Whitehead, L. (1986), 'Some International Aspects of Democratization', in O'Donnell *et al.*, Vol. III, *Comparative Perspectives*.

Wiarda, H.J. (ed.) (1980), *The Continuing Struggle for Democracy in Latin America*. Boulder CO: Westview.

Williamson, J.B. and Pampel, F.C. (1986), 'Politics, Class and Growth in Social Security Effort: A Cross National Analysis', *International Journal of Comparative Sociology*, 27, 15-27.

Wiseman, J. (1986), 'Urban Riots in West Africa 1977-85', *Journal of Modern African Studies*, 24 (3), 509-518.

Wiseman, J.A. (1977), 'Multi-partyism in Africa: The case of Botswana', *African Affairs*, 76 (302), January, 70-79.

World Bank (1987, 1988a, 1991), *World Development Reports*. New York: Oxford University Press.

World Bank (1988b), *Report on Adjustment Lending*. Washington DC: World Bank.

World Bank (1989a), *Africa's Adjustment, Recovery and Growth*. Washington DC: World Bank.

World Bank (1989b), *Sub-Saharan Africa: From Crisis to Sustainable Growth*. Washington DC: World Bank.

World Bank (1989c), *Adjustment Lending: An Evaluation of 10 years of Experience*. Washington DC: World Bank.

World Bank (1989d), *Strengthening Trade Policy Reform*, Vol. II, Washington DC: World Bank.

World Bank (1990a), 'Evaluation of Adjustment Lending', *Policy Research Series*, No. 14.

World Bank (1990b), *Growth, Aid and Debt*. Washington DC: World Bank.

Wunsch, J.S. and Olowu, D. (eds) (1990), *Failure of the Centralized State: Institutions and Self Governance in Africa*. Boulder CO:

Westview.

Young, C. (1981), *Ideology and Development in Africa*. New Haven CT: Yale University Press.

Young, C. (1988), 'The African State and Its Political Legacy', in Rothchild and Chazan.

Yueng-Yi, G. (1989), 'On the Political Economies of Export-oriented industrialization in Korea and Taiwan in Comparison, *Economics*, 30, 83-111.

Zolberg, A. (1966), *Creating Political Order: The Party-States of West Africa*, Chicago IL: Rand MacNally.

Zolberg, A. (1968), 'The Structure of Political Conflict in the New States of Tropical Africa', *American Political Science Review*, 62 (1), March, 70-87.